BASIC STUDIES IN SCIENCE

Discovering Our World

SCIENCE FOR THE MIDDLE GRADES

by WILBUR L. BEAUCHAMP

MARY MELROSE WILLIAMS

GLENN O. BLOUGH

1

SCOTT, FORESMAN AND COMPANY

Chicago, Atlanta, Dallas, New York

ACKNOWLEDGMENTS

FOR MANY SUGGESTIONS that were very helpful in making this edition of DISCOVERING OUR WORLD, BOOK ONE, the authors are much indebted to the supervisors and teachers who read the material critically. Among those who gave help, special thanks are due Miss Anna E. Burgess, Supervising Principal, Cleveland, Ohio; Dr. Joe Young West, Maryland State Teachers College, Towson, Maryland; Miss Winifred Barry, Elementary Supervisor, Oceanside, New York; Miss Dorothy Hunt, Elementary Supervisor, North Kansas City, Missouri; Miss Irene Thomas, formerly Principal, The Perry School, Ann Arbor, Michigan.

The drawings were made by Christine Chisholm, Raymond E. Craig, Chauncey Maltman, Fiore Mastri, and Leon L. Pray.

Acknowledgment is made to the following for permission to publish the photographs on indicated pages: Acme Newspictures, Inc., 21, 29, 56, 85, 110; M. B. Adrian & Sons X-Ray Co., 171; American Dental Association, 162; *American Home,* Dr. E. Laurence Palmer, 180, 181 (left); American Museum of Natural History, 70, 194, 206 (right); H. A. Atwell, 86; Carl Berger, 173; Better Light Better Sight Bureau, 163; Bristol-Myers Company, 75; L. W. Brownell, 20, 27, 28, 32 (left), 36, 40 (bottom), 41 (top, bottom), 43, 51 (left), 184, 185, 188 (left), 189 (right); Century Photos, Inc., 134 (left); J. C. Allen, 19; Lynwood M. Chace, 14 (bottom), 40 (top); *Chicago Daily News,* 52, 182; Chicago Natural History Museum, 62-63, 71, 72 (dog, frog, alligator), 186-187; *Chicago Sun,* 14 (top); Davey Tree Expert Co., 55, 204; A. Devaney, Inc., 176; John Ripley Forbes, 26; Ford Motor Co., 46; Ewing Galloway, 51 (right), 59, 152, 164, 195; Philip D. Gendreau, 7; G. A. Douglas, 64; General Biological Supply House, Inc., 72 (snake, fish, and chicken); Ferdinand S. Hirsh, 82; International News Photo, 136; Kaufmann and Fabry, 199; Keystone View Co., 37 (right), 54 (left), 208 (right), 212 (left); Harold M. Lambert, 15, 158, 161, 169, 179 (left); *Life,* 6, 66; Lowell Observatory, 131, 135; Minnesota Mining & Mfg. Co., 124; Mount Wilson Observatory, 90; Multifinish Mfg. Co., 142 (left); Samuel Myslis, 156; National Dairy Council, 172; National Foot Health Council, 171 (bottom); National Safety Council, 175, 177, 178; *Newsweek,* 92; Dr. E. Laurence Palmer, 181 (right); Edward Probert, 12, 13; William K. Reynolds, 8; H. Armstrong Roberts, 179 (right); James Sawders, 159; Science Service, 140; Hugh Spencer, 32 (right), 37 (left), 40 (center), 41 (center), 42, 44-45, 188 (right and center), 189 (left), 205, 212 (right); U. S. Forest Service, 206 (left); U. S. Steel Corporation Subsidiaries, 114; University of Chicago, 207; photo by H. A. Vandenbree, reprinted from *The Instructor,* December 1942, by permission of Miss Isobel Willcox and the F. A. Owen Publishing Co., 38; Yerkes Observatory, 93, 116, 121, 125, 126-127, 132, 134 (right).

1947   1952

CONTENTS

To the Boys and Girls Who Study This Book

FROM THIS BOOK you will discover many things about the world you live in. If you looked at the Contents on pages 3-5, you know that the book is about plants and animals, about your own body, about what makes day and night, about the stars, about magnets, and about many other things that you see every day.

You will discover some of these things by reading. Some of them you will discover by looking at the pictures. Some you will discover by *experimenting*. Experimenting means trying them out yourself. Some you will discover by looking about you. Stop, look, and listen. And you will discover that the things told in this book really happen in the world you live in. Will the children in the picture on this page discover something about their world?

Someone had to discover the things that are in this book. Some were discovered long ago by people who were interested in the world around them. They watched plants and animals growing. They watched the stars and the moon. They noticed things about the earth. They could not always explain the things they saw. But they discovered many of the things that we know about today.

Many of the things in this book were discovered by men and women called *scientists*. Scientists have learned ways of studying the things they see. They find out about them by examining them, by using instruments, and by experimenting. By using these ways, scientists can discover new things. And they can explain some of the things that people saw but did not understand.

On this page are pictures of two scientists at work. One is using an instrument called a *microscope* to look at something that is very, very small. The other is doing an experiment. He is *testing* buttons made of a new material. He wants to find out what happens to them when they are put into very hot water.

As these scientists work, they follow certain rules so that they can be sure that what they discover is really true. They work carefully to discover the answers to questions. They always examine things very carefully. They try experiments over and over before they believe what the experiments show. They think things over before they say what they believe.

When you use this book, you will learn more if you follow these rules. Try to read carefully, examine things with care, do the experiments just as the directions tell you to, and do not decide that a thing is true before you have thought carefully about it.

If you follow these rules, you will discover many things about the world you live in. You will learn what happens to a tadpole's tail, what happens to the sun at night, and why winter comes. You will find the answers to hundreds of other questions. It took scientists many years to discover the answers to these questions. You can discover them very easily for yourself by studying DISCOVERING OUR WORLD.

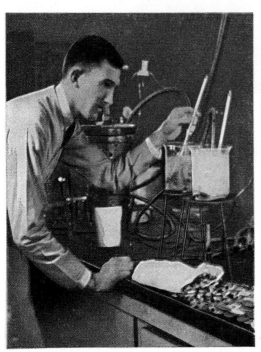

★ In Unit One You Will Learn ★

★ *What the two big groups of things are* ★ *How all living things are alike* ★ *How non-living things are alike* ★ *What the two biggest groups of living things are* ★ *How we can tell in what group a living thing belongs* ★ *What mammals, birds, reptiles, fish, amphibians, and other animals are* ★ ★ *What the two big groups of plants are* ★

★ UNIT 1 ★

How Are the Things of the World Put in Groups?

ON THE SECOND DAY of school Robert came hurrying home as fast as he could.

"Mother," he said, "is there any more of that wallboard that Dad used to make the room in the attic?"

"Yes," answered his mother, "there are some small pieces left, I'm sure. What do you want them for?"

"I want to get my butterflies ready so that I can take them to school tomorrow. Those soft boards will be just the thing. I can pin the butterflies to them easily. Our teacher wants us to bring anything we've collected outdoors. She said to bring pet animals, too, and some plants."

So Robert went to work with his butterflies. He found some cardboard boxes and sawed the wallboard to fit inside them. Then he pinned the butterflies to the boards and put them in the boxes.

Next morning Robert's mother helped him tie his boxes together so that he could carry them safely.

When he came into the schoolroom, the others in the class crowded around to see what he had. His teacher came to look at Robert's butterflies, too.

"You had better put them on the shelf, Robert," she said. "Everyone can see them easily there."

The other boys and girls had also brought things. "The rest of you may put your things there, too," the teacher said.

This shelf was about two feet wide and just high enough for the boys and girls to see everything that was on it. It was much like the shelf in the picture on page 11.

9

While the children were looking at Robert's butterflies, they asked him one question after another about them. He was glad he could answer so many of the questions. At last, John asked, "How did you learn so much about butterflies?"

"By watching them," answered Robert, "and by reading about butterflies in a book I got from the library."

Robert had told his classmates two of the best ways of learning about the things that we see around us every day. Watch things closely and read about them.

If you keep your eyes open, you will surely see many things that will interest you. You will want to ask questions about them. Your teacher will help you find answers to your questions. And books will answer questions for you, too. But you will want to find answers by yourself whenever you can. Your eyes, your ears, your fingers, and even your nose will help you find the answers to questions.

The next day more of the boys and girls brought things for the science shelf. They brought grasshoppers, a stuffed squirrel, white rats, stones, a crayfish, colored glass, a clam shell, snails, snakes, plants, and many other things they had collected.

What are the two big groups of things?

"IF YOU PUT these things in some order, it will be much easier to learn about them," said the teacher one day. "We have the snakes next to the stones, the butterflies next to the white rats, and the grasshoppers beside the stuffed squirrel. I think we should put them in some kind of order."

"I know what you mean," said John. "My father keeps different sizes of nails in separate boxes, and he has other boxes with a different kind of thing in each box. I know just where to look when I want to find a big nail or a little tack."

"That's good, John," said the teacher. "But what should we do with all our things to put the shelf in order?"

"Oh, I know," said John. "Let's put the things that are like each other together."

John's plan was a good one. It is the way scientists work. They separate things into different groups. Each group is made up of things that are like each other. So the boys and girls looked carefully at all the things. They began to think about why some of the things belonged together and why some did not belong together.

Here are the things the children in one science class brought to school. Someone even brought a pet porcupine!

Nancy was the first one to speak. "The rocks and glass don't belong with my cat and kitten," she said. "The cat and kitten are alive, but rocks and glass are not alive."

"That is a good way to begin," said the teacher. "We can put all the *living things* into one group and all the *non-living things* in another group."

All the things in the world can be divided into these two groups: *living things* and *non-living things.* A living thing is something that is alive now or that was alive at one time. When we say a thing is a non-living thing, we mean that it never was alive. Rocks and glass are things that never were alive.

1. What are two good ways of learning about the world we live in? Tell something that you have learned this week by using these two ways.
2. What do your eyes, ears, fingers, and nose tell you about things?
3. Why did the teacher ask the children to bring many things to school?
4. Why is it a good idea to put things in groups?
5. Try to name ten living things and ten non-living things. Keep your lists. After you have read more in this unit, you can check them to see if they are correct.

The pictures on these two pages were taken while this magnolia flower was opening. The pictures on this page show the tight bud and how it looked one hour later.

How are all living things alike?

THE BOYS AND GIRLS looked closely at a few things that they knew were living things—the cat and kitten, the snails, the stuffed squirrel, and the butterflies. The cat and kitten and the snails were alive, and the stuffed squirrel and the butterflies were once alive. Then the class started thinking and talking about how all these were alike. As they talked, the teacher wrote on the blackboard what they said about living things. This is the list she made.

1. Living things can move.
2. Living things can breathe.
3. Living things need food.
4. Living things can grow.
5. Living things can have young like themselves.

When she finished writing, the teacher said, "All living things can move, can breathe, need food, can grow, and can have young like themselves. Suppose you put each living thing at one end of the science shelf. But first, you must tell the class why you think each thing belongs to the group of living things."

"My cat and kitten are certainly living things," Nancy said. "They can move, and they breathe. They need food, too. I give them milk three times a day. And the kitten has grown, too. Cats can have young like themselves, for the cat is the kitten's mother."

The other boys and girls agreed with Nancy that the cat and kitten should be put with the living things.

The left-hand picture on this page was taken only fifteen minutes after the right-hand one on page 12. Forty-five minutes later the flower was open wide.

"My snakes are living things," said Henry. "They move so fast it's hard to catch them if they get out of the cage. Of course, they can breathe. They need food, too, and they have grown. Snakes can have young like themselves, for these baby snakes came from eggs that were laid by a snake."

Henry put the cage of snakes with the living things. And, one by one, the boys and girls picked out the living things and moved them to one end of the shelf.

Then Betty began to wonder if the petunia plant was a living thing. She could not see that the plant moved or breathed.

Perhaps you are like Betty and think that plants do not move and breathe. Of course, plants have no legs or wings with which they can move about from place to place. But if you saw a slow-motion picture of plants growing, you would be surprised. You would see stems shooting up and out, and buds swelling. You would see flowers opening as the magnolia flower in the pictures is doing. Then you would know that plants move as they grow.

Although a plant does not have a nose, it breathes in air. Later in this book, you will learn how plants breathe. You will also find out that plants need to have food to make them grow.

Betty knew that the petunia plant could produce other petunias because she had raised the plant from seed. She knew that the seed had come from full-grown petunia plants. So

she put the petunia plant with the living things. All plants are living things.

"Do these leaves from an oak tree belong with the living things?" asked Helen.

"Yes," explained the teacher, "they were parts of a tree. And a tree, you know, is a living thing. A piece of wood should also be put with the living things because at one time it was a part of a tree, too."

The class then put a feather, a snakeskin, some flowers, some pine cones, some snail shells, and a clam shell with the group of living things. Each of them was once a part of a living thing.

---

1. *In what ways are all living things alike?*
2. *Which of these would you put in the group of living things?*
   Fur   Leather   Paper   Glass   Hair   Bone   Iron
3. *Was your list of living things correct? How do you know?*
4. *The large zebra is the mother of the little one. The baby snakes came from eggs laid by a mother snake. Are zebras and snakes living things?*

How are all non-living things alike?

TO HELP THE BOYS and girls find out about non-living things, the teacher suggested that they compare a man with a snowman.

They knew that a man is a living thing. He can move and breathe. He needs food, has grown, and can have children. But the snowman cannot move itself, cannot breathe, cannot take in food, cannot grow, and cannot have young like itself. They decided that the snowman must be a non-living thing.

The class also compared a live duck with a toy duck made of metal. The toy duck cannot move, cannot breathe, does not need to eat food, cannot grow into a larger toy duck, and cannot have young toy ducks. Then the boys and girls knew that the live duck is a living thing but that the metal toy duck is a non-living thing.

The teacher wrote on the blackboard what the class had found out about non-living things.

1. Non-living things cannot move.
2. Non-living things cannot breathe.
3. Non-living things do not need food.
4. Non-living things cannot grow.
5. Non-living things cannot have young like themselves.

How is a snowman different from a real man?

Henry picked up one of the stones in his collection. Of course, he knew it was a non-living thing. It did not eat food or breathe air. It would never grow from a small stone into a big stone. It could not produce more stones like itself, and it could not move itself.

Henry said that you could leave a stone by the side of a tree for years. The tree would grow larger, but the stone would not get bigger.

"A piece of glass has no eyes or ears, and it has no nose or mouth," said Peggy. "Non-living things can't see, hear, smell, feel, or eat."

A book, a vase, a glass, and a pair of scissors were some of the things the children put with the group of non-living things.

At last, the boys and girls had all of their things in two groups. They made one cardboard sign that said LIVING THINGS and put it at the end of the shelf where all the living things were. Another sign said NON-LIVING THINGS. This was put up in front of the non-living group.

1. *In what five ways are living things different from non-living things?*
2. *What does* non-living *mean?*
3. *Separate the things in the picture on this page into living things and non-living things.*
4. *Make a list of all the living things in the pictures in this unit.*
5. *Make a list of all the non-living things in the pictures in this unit.*
6. *Look at the list of non-living things you made to answer the question on page 11. Was the list correct? How do you know?*

What are the two biggest groups of living things?

BETTY NOW LOOKED at the two groups and said, "It didn't take long to get everything put in order, did it?"

But Betty did not know that the class had only just started. A scientist knows that everything in the world is either living or non-living. But a scientist needs to know more than that. He must know the different kinds of living things and the different kinds of non-living things.

"We can separate all living things into two big groups," said the teacher. "Will you look at the living things on the shelf? See if you can find out for yourselves what the two groups are."

"Well, my white rats and Helen's geranium plant don't belong together," said Charley. "I think the two groups must be plants and animals."

Charley was right. Every living thing is either a plant or an animal. So the class went to work, dividing their living things into the two groups. Of course, they had no trouble telling which things were plants and which were animals.

While the boys and girls were separating the plants and animals, Nancy began to be puzzled about something.

"We are certainly alive," she said. "So we must be either plants or ani-

How are the white rats different from the geranium plant?

Which of the living things in this picture are plants? Which ones belong to the animal group?

mals. I know I am not a plant. Am I an animal?"

"Well, Nancy," answered the teacher, "you and I are living things, aren't we? We must belong in either the plant group or the animal group. You know that we are not plants. So you and I and all other people must belong in the same big group of living things as the animals belong in."

The boys and girls laughed. They said they did not know before that they were in the same group as cats, dogs, birds, and other animals. Soon they had all of the plants and animals on the shelf divided into two groups. They made two more signs. One sign read PLANTS. The other sign read ANIMALS. They put each sign with the group to which it belonged.

---

1. *How do you tell whether a living thing is a plant or an animal?*
2. *Make a list of all the plants shown in the pictures in this unit.*
3. *Make a list of all the animals shown in the pictures in this unit.*

Are the cat and the chicken made alike?

How can we tell what group an animal belongs in?

WHEN THE CLASS came in one morning, the teacher said, "Our next job is to divide all our animals into different groups and our plants into different groups. That is what a scientist does, and this is how he does it. A scientist studies things to see how they are made. He says, 'If they are made alike, they belong together. If they are not made alike, they do not belong together.' Are all the animals on the science shelf made alike?"

"Well, the snakes certainly aren't made like the rats," said Henry.

"That's easy to see," said John. "The rats have hair, and they walk on legs. The snakes have no hair on them, and they slide along on their stomachs. They aren't made like rats."

Then the boys and girls began to talk about all the differences they could find in the ways animals are made. They thought of two-legged animals, four-legged animals, and even eight-legged animals. They named animals that have no legs, some that have fins, and some that have wings. They had seen animals covered with hair, animals covered with feathers, animals covered with smooth skin like a frog's, and animals covered with shells.

Scientists have a word that they use when they talk about the way anything is made. The word is *structure*. Structure means the parts of a thing and how the parts are put together. Studying different animals will help you see what structure means.

How is a squirrel's structure different from a frog's?

How many differences can you find between the structure of a chicken and the structure of a cat? Before you can answer this question, you must know what parts a cat has and what parts a chicken has. Make a list of the parts of each animal. Then look at your lists and see what the differences in structure are. Here are the lists the class made. What differences in structure did they see when they looked at their lists?

A Cat's Structure	*A Chicken's Structure*
1. Four legs	1. Two legs
2. Hair	2. Feathers
3. Teeth	3. Two wings
4. Mouth and lips	4. A bill
5. A nose	5. Holes in the bill for a nose
6. Ears that stick out	6. Holes in the head for ears

---

1. *How are horses and dogs alike? How are they different?*
2. *How is the structure of a fish different from the structure of a bird?*
3. *How would you describe your own structure?*
4. *Why is it important for a scientist to know about the structure of an animal?*
5. *Choose an animal in one of the pictures in this unit and describe its structure. Do not tell your class which animal you have chosen. Try to describe its structure so carefully that they can guess which animal it is.*

What is a mammal?

"WE HAVE a good collection of animals here on our science shelf," said the teacher one morning. "And they belong to many different groups. Look at the cat, the white rats, and the rabbit. Think about their parts and then try to tell how these animals are alike."

John was the first one to answer. "Well," he said, "every one of these animals has four legs and two eyes."

"That's good, John," said the teacher, "but so does the frog. Do you think that the frog belongs to the same group as the cat, the rats, and the rabbit?"

John was not sure. Do you think the frog belongs with the cat, the rats, and the rabbit? Later on, you will learn with what group the frog belongs.

"Is there any other way the cat, the rabbit, and the rats are alike?" asked the teacher.

Quickly Mary spoke up. "They all are covered with fur," she said.

Mary had noticed an important thing. Fur or hair is one way that scientists tell this group of animals from all other groups. They call the animals in this group *mammals*. All mammals are covered with fur or hair, or else they have hair somewhere on their bodies.

As the children were looking at the animals, Peggy said, "Oh, look at the little kitten getting its dinner from the mother cat!"

Peggy had found another way in which all mammals are alike. Young mammals get milk from their mothers' bodies. Mammals are the only animals that feed their babies this way. All baby mammals are raised on milk.

These are two ways in which mammals are different from all other animals.

1. They have fur or hair.
2. They feed milk to their babies.

Is the giraffe a mammal? How do you know?

ARMADILLO

RED FOX

CHIPMUNK

WOODCHUCK

SKUNK

MEADOW MOUSE

All of the animals on these two pages are mammals—even the strange-looking armadillo.

Then the teacher told the class two more very important things about mammals. First, she told them that mammals are *warm-blooded*. Do you know what warm-blooded means?

The temperature of the blood of a warm-blooded animal stays about the same all the time. You are warm-blooded. You may feel cold on a cold winter day, but your blood is as warm as it is on a hot day. On a hot day you may feel very warm, but your blood is no warmer than it is on a cold day.

The blood of every mammal stays at almost the same temperature all the time. So we say that mammals are warm-blooded.

The other important thing about mammals is the way they get air. Every living thing must have air to stay alive. But not all living things get air into their bodies in the same way. Mammals have *lungs*. When a mammal breathes, the air goes in through the mouth or nose and down into the lungs. The lungs help get the air into the body where it is used. Mammals must live in the air. Or if they live in the water, they must come up to the surface quite often to get air into their lungs.

So the children had learned four things that are true about all animals in the mammal group. These four things are listed on the next page.

Which of these mammals have you ever seen or read about?

1. Mammals have fur or hair.
2. The babies are fed with milk from their mothers' bodies.
3. Mammals are warm-blooded.
4. Mammals take air into their bodies with lungs.

The teacher then asked the boys and girls to look carefully to see if they could find some other mammals in the room besides the rabbit, the rats, and the cat.

The children looked and looked. At last, Robert said, "I know. We are mammals."

Robert was right. We have hair. Our mothers can feed their babies with milk from their own bodies. We are warm-blooded, and we have lungs.

---

1. *Which of these animals are mammals? How do you know?*
   Dog   Horse   Frog   Cow   Snake   Crow   Beaver   Lion
2. *Find all the pictures of mammals shown in this unit.*
3. *Why is it incorrect to say that mammals are animals with four feet?*
4. *How is a mammal like any other living thing? How is it different from any other living thing that is not a mammal?*
5. *Try to find out which mammals live in water.*

MAGPIE

PARROT

HUMMINGBIRD

BALTIMORE ORIOLE

BOBWHITE

PUFFIN

Some birds are very large. Some are very small. Some have strange shapes. But they all have the parts that show you they are birds.

How are birds different from other animals?

IT WAS EASY for the class to find out the important things about the structure of birds. Of course, they had all seen many different kinds of birds. They could look out of the schoolroom window and see bluejays, sparrows, and robins. Every bird they could think of had two wings, two legs, and feathers. They decided that all birds have this structure.

There is another important thing that the children noticed about the structure of birds. Do you know what the difference is between the mouths of birds and the mouths of other animals?

"When we looked at the chicken," said Peggy, "we saw that it didn't have any teeth. And I'm sure my canary has no teeth. The chicken and the canary have hard bills. They can use their bills to pick up food and crack seeds."

Peggy had discovered another important thing about birds. Birds do not have any teeth.

"Are birds warm-blooded like mammals?" asked Mary.

WILD TURKEY

OSTRICH

MALLARD DUCK

HORNED OWL

PELICAN

LYRE BIRD

FLAMINGO

Do the birds in these pictures all have the same kind of bills? What different kinds of legs and feet can you find?

"Yes, Mary," answered the teacher, "birds are warm-blooded. On a cold day as well as on a warm day the temperature of a bird's blood is always warm. Birds are warm-blooded animals."

Then the teacher told the class another thing to remember about the structure of birds. All birds breathe with lungs.

The class was now ready to write on the blackboard the important things they had learned about the structure of birds.

1. Birds are covered with feathers.
2. Birds have two wings and two legs.
3. Birds have bills.
4. Birds are warm-blooded.
5. Birds breathe with lungs.

---

1. *How are birds like mammals? How are they different from mammals?*
2. *Is a duck a bird? How do you know?*
3. *Is a bee a bird? How do you know?*

The children are learning how to handle this harmless Indigo snake. This kind of snake makes an interesting pet and helps us by catching rats.

How are all reptiles alike?

So FAR THE CLASS had discovered two animal groups — the mammals and the birds. They began to see that putting all the animals of the world into groups was quite a job. They discovered that they had to know a great deal about the parts of animals.

"What animals shall we study next?" asked Henry. "I'd like to know about my snakes. What group do they belong in?"

"You caught the snakes, Henry," replied his teacher, "and you have had plenty of chances to study them. What can you tell us about the structure of snakes?"

"Well," said Henry, "they haven't any legs or wings, and they are not covered with feathers or hair."

"Let's look closely at your snakes," said the teacher, "and find out what they are covered with."

So the boys and girls crowded around the box while Henry took out one of his snakes. He took hold of it just back of the neck and handled it very gently and carefully.

You must always be careful with snakes, just as you must be careful with any wild animal. Never disturb a snake when it is eating. When you pick up a snake, hold it just back of the head so it cannot bite you. Even though the snake is not poisonous, its bite could cause you trouble. Never get near a snake unless you are sure that it is not poisonous. If you are careful to follow these rules, you may enjoy having snakes as pets.

As the boys and girls looked at the snake carefully, Peggy said, "Why, it is covered all over with little *scales!*"

Then the teacher showed the children a big snakeskin that had been sent to the school. On this skin the boys and girls could plainly see the thin, flat scales. These fitted over each other like shingles on a roof. The class had discovered an important thing about another group of animals. The animals in this group are called *reptiles.* A snake is a reptile.

The class was just about ready to decide that all reptiles have scales like the scales on a snake. But the teacher said, "Let's look at another reptile before we decide."

She went over to where one of the boys had made a home for his turtles. "Are there any scales on this animal?" she asked, as she picked up one of the turtles and gave it to Billy to hold.

"Why, is this a reptile?" asked Billy. "It has legs, but snakes haven't."

You can plainly see the scales on this snake.

Can you see why a turtle belongs to the same group of animals as a snake?

"Yes," replied the teacher, "the turtle is a reptile. Reptiles have either very short legs or no legs at all."

"Well," said Billy, "I don't see any scales, but it has a hard shell."

When the children looked at the shell, they were surprised to find that it was made of scales. But these scales are different from those on the snake. The scales of the turtle fit together so closely that they seem to make one hard piece.

All reptiles have scales. A turtle has little scales on its legs and neck. Alligators, crocodiles, lizards, snakes, and turtles are all reptiles. They all have scales.

While the class was studying the snakes and turtles, Henry asked, "Are snakes, turtles, and other reptiles warm-blooded?"

"No, Henry," answered his teacher. "Snakes are not warm-blooded animals. They are *cold-blooded.*"

Then she explained what cold-blooded really means. It means that the animal's blood changes temperature when the temperature around the animal changes. When a snake is sunning itself on a rock, its blood is warm. But when the snake is in a cold hole in the ground, its blood is cold. All reptiles are cold-blooded.

"How do reptiles breathe?" asked Peggy. "Do they have lungs?"

"Yes, they have lungs just as birds and mammals have," answered the teacher. "Some reptiles live on land all the time, and others live in water all the time. Some live in the water part of the time and on land part of the time. But all reptiles breathe with lungs. Those that live in water must come up to the surface for air."

Now the class was ready to write **on** the blackboard the important things they had learned about the structure of reptiles.

1. Reptiles are covered with scales or a shell made of scales.
2. Reptiles have either very short legs or no legs at all.
3. Reptiles are cold-blooded.
4. Reptiles breathe with lungs.

---

1. *What are two ways in which reptiles are different from birds and mammals?*
2. *What is one way in which reptiles are like birds and mammals?*
3. *Which of these statements are right?*
   a) *Snakes have scales.*
   b) *All reptiles have legs.*
   c) *Snakes have a different structure from birds.*
4. *What is the difference between* warm-blooded *and* cold-blooded?
5. *What rules should you remember so that you can enjoy having snakes for pets?*

Look at the picture and tell why these crocodiles are put in the reptile group.

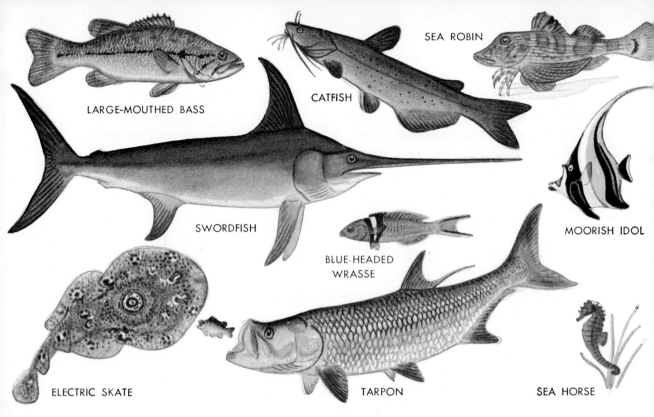

There are many, many different kinds of fish. Some of them may not look much like fish, but they all have the same parts that every fish has.

LARGE-MOUTHED BASS

CATFISH

SEA ROBIN

SWORDFISH

BLUE-HEADED WRASSE

MOORISH IDOL

ELECTRIC SKATE

TARPON

SEA HORSE

How are all fish alike?

JOHN HAD BEEN on a fishing trip with his father just before school opened. He had seen three kinds of fish—perch, bass, and sunfish. He helped catch them, clean them, and eat them. So he had learned many things about them. One day in class he said, "I think fish must be reptiles. They are covered with scales, and I think they must be cold-blooded."

"You are partly right," said the teacher. "All fish are cold-blooded, and nearly all of them are covered with scales. But fish are not reptiles. Let's look at these goldfish. What

can you see on the fish that you can't see on a snake?"

Peggy was quick to answer, "Fins."

"Yes," said the teacher, "fish have fins. Can you see any other difference between the snakes and the fish?"

"I know," said John. "Fish have *gills*. I kept my fish on a string that I put through their gills and out through their mouths. Why do fish make their gills go in and out all the time, as these goldfish do?"

"The parts that you see going in and out are really covers for the gills," explained the teacher. "The gills are soft, thin parts under these covers. As the covers move in and out, water can go in and out over the gills."

Then the children watched the gill covers of a goldfish move in and out, in and out, as it breathed. The picture on this page shows you a fish's gills, too.

"Fish breathe through their gills," the teacher went on. "There is air in water. Fish can get the air from the water with their gills. All living things must breathe. You know that many animals breathe with lungs, but fish breathe with their gills."

The class then wrote on the blackboard the important things about the structure of fish.

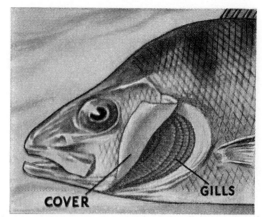

The gill cover has been turned back to show the gills.

1. Fish are usually covered with scales.
2. Fish have fins.
3. Fish are cold-blooded.
4. Fish breathe with gills.

---

1. *In what way is the structure of a fish different from the structures of the other groups of animals you have studied?*
2. *What are two ways in which fish and reptiles are alike?*
3. *In what two ways are reptiles and fish different?*

What are amphibians?

ONE DAY BILLY came to school much excited. "Come and see what I have in this box!" he called.

The boys and girls gathered close to see, but not one of them could name the animal that was in the box.

They asked their teacher to tell them what it was. But she only said, "Look at its structure, and perhaps you can find out what group it belongs in."

When the boys and girls looked at this new animal, they saw that its body was not covered with fur or hair or feathers. They said that they thought maybe it was a reptile. But they could not find any scales or a shell on it. Then Nancy said, "I think

The animal on the left is a toad. The one on the right is a salamander.

it's most like our frog. Anyway, it has a smooth, shiny skin like the frog's skin."

Nancy was right. The frog and the new animal belong in the same group. They are both *amphibians*.

The boys and girls looked through a book that told about amphibians. They found the picture of Billy's animal and learned that it was called a *salamander*.

Then the class began to look carefully at the frog and the salamander to find out for themselves all they could about the structure of amphibians. In the book about amphibians they learned that **when** an amphibian is young, it lives in the water and breathes with gills. When it grows older, it breathes with lungs and can live on land. Amphibians have no hair, no feathers, and no scales or shells. They are also cold-blooded. Toads, frogs, and salamanders belong in this group of animals. They are all amphibians.

These are the important things the class found out about amphibians.

1. Amphibians breathe with gills when young and with lungs when grown up.
2. Amphibians are covered only with skin.
3. Amphibians are cold-blooded.

---

1. *Which two ways of discovering did the boys and girls use? Have you used these ways as you studied this unit?*
2. *How are amphibians like fish and reptiles?*
3. *How are amphibians different from fish and reptiles?*

How are all insects alike?

FOR SEVERAL DAYS Robert had wanted to know where his butterflies belonged. At last, the teacher said, "Today, Robert, we will begin to study your butterflies and the other animals that belong with them. Let's see how crickets, grasshoppers, ants, bees, and butterflies are alike. These animals belong in the group called *insects.*"

"We will learn about the grasshoppers, the ants, the crickets, and Robert's butterflies at the same time. You may not think that they belong together. But when you study their structure, you will see why they do."

The class had enough insects in the cages and jars so that each boy and girl could study one of them. Some of the insects were dead, but that only made it easier to study their structure. Some of the live insects were put in small glass jars so that the class could watch them move.

Before the class began, the teacher wrote these questions on the blackboard for the class to answer.

1. How many legs does the animal have?
2. How many parts has its body?
3. How many feelers does it have?
4. What is its body covered with?
5. How does it breathe?

At last, the boys and girls were ready to tell what they had found. Betty told about the grasshoppers. She said, "A grasshopper has six legs. When we looked on the underside of the grasshopper, we could see three parts to its body. It seems to have some kind of covering over its body. We could see four wings. There are two feelers that stick out from its head."

Then John told about his ants. "An ant has six legs, too," he said. "You can see three parts to its body. And there are two feelers on its head. But my ants do not have wings."

Look at the picture on this page. You can see the parts that the children found on their insects.

The three parts of an insect's body have names. The part numbered 1 in the picture is its *head.* The middle part, numbered 2, is called the *thorax.* The part numbered 3 is called the *abdomen.*

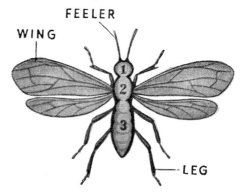

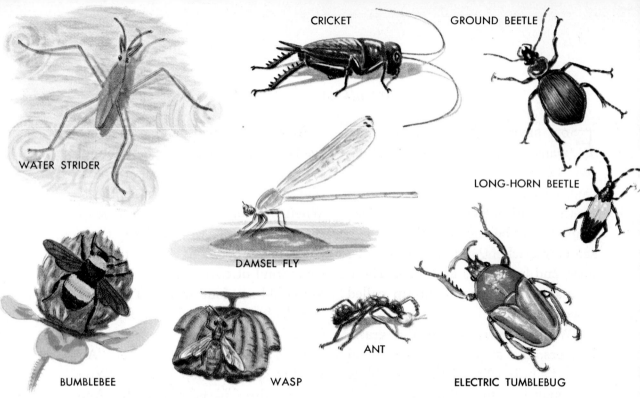

WATER STRIDER

CRICKET

GROUND BEETLE

LONG-HORN BEETLE

DAMSEL FLY

ANT

BUMBLEBEE

WASP

ELECTRIC TUMBLEBUG

There are more animals in the insect group than in any other. These are just a few of the many different kinds of insects.

An insect's feeler has a name, too. It is called an *antenna*. When we talk about two feelers, we say *antennae*.

The structure of these six-legged animals that the class was studying is quite different from the structure of the other animals they had studied. The body of every insect is divided into three parts. Ants plainly show these three parts. Some insects, though, have the head and middle part closely joined together. You would need to use a magnifying glass to see the three parts.

The legs of all insects are fastened to the thorax. If the insect has wings, they are fastened to the thorax, too.

One of the most interesting things about insects is that they have no bones. Mammals, birds, reptiles, amphibians, and fish have a *skeleton* of bones on the inside of their bodies. This is a framework that helps hold the soft parts of the body together and gives an animal its shape.

Insects have a covering on the outside of their bodies. This covering takes the place of the skeleton of bones that mammals and many other animals have. On some insects the covering is almost as hard as your fingernails. On others it is very thin. Beetles have a very hard covering on their bodies. A mosquito's covering is much thinner.

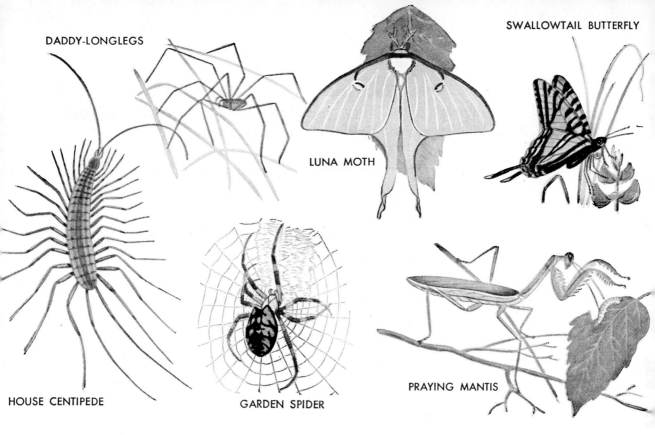

DADDY-LONGLEGS

SWALLOWTAIL BUTTERFLY

LUNA MOTH

HOUSE CENTIPEDE

GARDEN SPIDER

PRAYING MANTIS

You can hunt for some of these animals in your own back yard or in the park.

Henry had been holding a grasshopper under a magnifying glass. At last, he said, "What is this little row of dots along the sides of the grasshopper?"

"Those little dots are breathing holes," said the teacher. "The grasshopper gets air through them. All insects breathe in this way. Mammals breathe with lungs. So do birds, reptiles, and amphibians. Fish breathe with gills. But insects get air into their bodies through the many breathing holes along the sides of their bodies."

Then the class named the ways all insects are alike.

1. Insects have six legs.
2. Insects have two feelers.
3. Insects have a body that is divided into three parts.
4. Insects have a covering on the outside of their bodies.
5. Insects breathe through breathing holes along the sides of their bodies.

Read over this list of the ways in which all insects are alike and look at the pictures on this page. Are all of these animals insects? You are probably surprised to find out that the spider and the daddy-longlegs cannot be put with the insects. As you can see, a spider and a daddy-longlegs have more than six legs. Their bodies are divided into two parts. They belong in another group of animals.

Do you think a centipede is an insect? Or do you think it belongs in another group, too?

---

1. *Name five ways in which all insects are alike.*
2. *How do insects breathe?*
3. *Which of these ways did the boys and girls use to find the answers to their questions?*

   Thinking   Reading   Asking   Watching
4. *Use each of these ways to find out if a bee is an insect.*
5. *Why is a spider not put into the insect group?*
6. *Name all the insects you can think of that live near your school.*

Are there other groups of animals?

THE CHILDREN had learned that a spider is not an insect because a spider has eight legs and its body is divided into two parts. But the spider did not belong in any of the other animal groups the children had learned about.

The children looked again at their science shelf. They found that there were still several animals that they

SNAIL

CRAYFISH

had not put into any group. The snail and the clam and the crayfish did not belong in any of the groups they had named.

Two of the children had been to the seashore. They had brought back some starfish and a prickly animal called a sea urchin. These did not fit into any of the animal groups. There were also some earthworms that had not been put in any group of animals.

"Where shall we put all these other animals?" asked Nancy.

"That is a good question," replied the teacher. "There are other groups of animals you have not learned about. These other groups of animals are all alike in one important way.

They have no skeleton of bones inside their bodies. The animals you are wondering about belong in these other groups of animals. You will learn the names of these other groups and more about them later on in your science work. Mammals, birds, fish, reptiles, amphibians, and insects are the most common groups of animals. Suppose we put all the other animals together and just call them other animal groups."

At last, the class had put all the animals into groups. They made a sign for each group.

MAMMALS   FISH   AMPHIBIANS
BIRDS   REPTILES   INSECTS
OTHER ANIMAL GROUPS

The animal in the left-hand picture is a starfish. The other picture shows a sea urchin. The children in the picture on page 6 will probably find animals like these in the pools among the rocks.

	Name	Leaf length	Cluster	Shade	Stem	Uses	Other facts
1	white pine	3' to 5'	5	bluish green		fuel, houses	4 cones
2	c	scaly		light		shingles land-scaping	
3		$\frac{1}{2}$ to $\frac{3}{4}$	pointing every direction	pale			needly

These children are learning about some evergreen trees by studying their parts and describing how they look.

What are the two big groups of plants?

Now ALL the animals on the science shelf were separated into groups. But the plants were all together just as the children had placed them. What would you do if someone asked you to put a lot of different plants in groups?

"Plants are different from each other," said Betty. "We can look at them and see how they are made. We can do the same things that helped us put our animals into groups."

"Yes," said the teacher, "let us study the plants carefully. Perhaps we can find some differences in structure that will help us put them in groups. Of course, you know that plants are not covered with feathers or fur. And they do not have arms or legs or wings or eyes. But they do have parts, just as animals have parts. Structure, you know, means the parts of anything and the way they are put together."

The teacher showed the class a snapdragon plant she had pulled up from her garden that morning.

The boys and girls pointed out some of its parts. They found the *roots*, the *stems*, the *leaves*, and the *flowers*. Which of these parts can you find in the picture of the bean plant?

There was one other part of the plant that the boys and girls were not sure about. This part was brown, and it seemed to be some kind of *pod*. Mary was sure it had come from a flower. It grew on the plant in the place where the flower had been. The

class opened the pod, and they found little black seeds inside.

Then the teacher explained that every kind of plant that has flowers also has seeds. The seeds are formed inside the flower. The flower withers away, and the seeds are left to fall to the ground and grow into new plants.

"This afternoon when you get home," she said, "look for some flowers that have made seeds and bring the plants to school tomorrow."

Billy brought a bean plant from his father's garden. He showed it to the class and said, "You can see the roots, the stem, the leaves, a flower, and a bean pod. The seeds are the beans inside the bean pod. And here is a tiny bean pod that is just starting to grow from the flower."

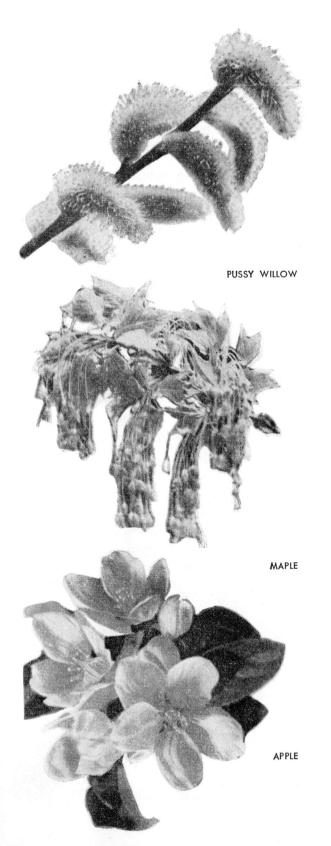

PUSSY WILLOW

MAPLE

APPLE

The next day Nancy brought a sunflower that had many seeds in it. All the children looked at the flower carefully.

"Do all plants have seeds?" Henry asked.

"No," answered the teacher, "some plants do not have seeds."

The answer to the question showed the class the first thing to do in putting the plants in groups. They had to divide their plants into two big groups. So their teacher helped them divide all their plants into these two groups.

1. Plants that have seeds.

2. Plants that do not have seeds.

As soon as the class had done this, they began to name some of the plants they knew that grow from seeds. They named sweet peas, petunias, peas, beans, asters, pansies, and many others in their gardens.

Perhaps you think that flowers are always large, with bright colors. But when a scientist uses the word *flower*, he means the part of a plant that grows seeds.

Maple trees have flowers. So do beech, hickory, and walnut trees. Their flowers are small, and you probably have never noticed them. You eat the seeds of some of these trees, but you call them nuts.

"You certainly can see the flowers on apple trees and horse-chestnut trees and locust trees," said Nancy. "And you can smell them, too."

"Then grass must have flowers, too," said Henry. "We planted grass seed in our yard this spring."

Henry was right. Grass has flowers, too, but they are so tiny you probably have never seen them. Corn tassels are really flowers, and the tops of wheat plants have tiny flowers.

"Now let us learn about plants that have no flowers and no seeds," said the teacher. "First, let's look at Betty's fern. Did you ever see flowers on a fern? I'm sure you never did, for a fern does not have either flowers or seeds."

Then she showed the class the underside of a fern leaf. There were rows of little yellow-brown dots on it, just like the ones in the picture on this page. The class studied the dots on the fern leaf carefully. They found that they could break the dots open. When the dots were broken open, something that looked like brown dust came out. The teacher told the children that each tiny bit of this dust could grow into a new plant.

The children knew that seeds grow into new plants. But they said that the bits of brown dust did not look at all like the apple seeds, bean seeds, and other seeds they had seen. And they were right. The bits of dust are not seeds. They are called *spores*.

BLACK WALNUT

FERN

PUFFBALLS

41

"This mushroom doesn't have any flowers or seeds," said Betty, after she had looked at it carefully. "Are there other kinds of plants that have spores instead of seeds?"

"Yes," answered the teacher, "if you crush one of these puffballs, you will see many spores. A puffball is a kind of mushroom, too. Puffballs and other mushrooms belong in the group of plants that grow from spores instead of seeds."

The boys and girls then looked at some moss. They saw many small plants growing very close together.

"These plants are very tiny, and they don't seem to have leaves and stems," Nancy said. "Moss plants have no flowers or seeds, have they?"

This beautiful mushroom is very poisonous. People who gather mushrooms to eat must know just which ones to pick.

"No," answered the teacher, "moss plants have no leaves and stems. And they have no flowers or seeds. They grow from spores, too."

The class learned that puffballs and other mushrooms, mosses, and ferns have no flowers or seeds. But they found out that all of these plants have spores.

Then the children looked at some seaweeds that they had brought from the seashore. Mary said, "We saw lots of seaweeds growing on the rocks and in the water. But we didn't see any flowers or seeds on them."

"Seaweeds belong to the group of plants that do not have flowers or seeds," explained the teacher. "Like ferns, mosses, and mushrooms, they have spores instead of seeds."

Now the boys and girls were ready to separate their collection of plants into two groups on the science shelf. The children made two signs.

HAVE FLOWERS AND SEEDS

HAVE NO FLOWERS AND NO SEEDS

They had very little trouble separating the plants until they came to the cone from a pine tree. They did not know whether pine trees grew from seeds. While Peggy was handling the cone, some seeds fell out of it. Then the children learned that this cone was the part of the pine tree that grew seeds. If the seeds are

The green pine cones are still growing, and the seeds are growing inside them. The brown ones have opened and dropped their seeds to the ground.

planted, little pine trees will grow from them.

All the plants with seeds are divided into two groups. One group grows its seeds in flowers. The other group grows its seeds in cones. Pines, spruces, firs, and hemlocks are trees that grow their seeds in cones.

---

1. Which groups of words below tell you something about the structure of a plant?

   a) Grows in the water
   b) Has red flowers
   c) Needs plenty of sunlight
   d) Lives only one year
   e) Has roots, stems, and leaves
   f) Has a short, thick root
   g) Is good to eat
   h) Has big, thick leaves
   i) Has seeds and flowers
   j) Has spores

2. In what parts of plants do the seeds grow?
3. Make a list of all the plants named in pages 38-43. Then divide them into two groups: *Plants with Seeds* and *Plants without Seeds*.

ANIMALS

BIRDS FISH MAMMALS REPTILES AMPHIBIANS INSE

LIVING THINGS

This is the way the science shelf looked when the class had finished putting all the things in the groups to which they belong.

QUESTIONS TO ANSWER

1. Suppose you had a collection of different kinds of buttons. How would you go about putting them into groups?

2. What do scientists do when they put things into groups?

3. How are insects different from the other animals you have studied?

4. If you found an insect that had wings, would it be correct to say that all insects have wings? Explain your answer.

5. If you found an animal in the woods and wanted to know in what group it belonged, how would you find out?

6. First, separate the things in the next column into *Living Things* and *Non-Living Things*. Then write the names of the plant groups and animal groups you have studied and put each living thing in the group where it belongs.

Mouse	Peach tree
Nail	Turkey
Cricket	Sheep
Toad	Pen point
Geranium	Duck
Mushroom	Paper clip
Rock	Grasshopper
Bottle	Salmon
Moss	Alligator
Snake	Frog
Sunfish	Pine tree
Penguin	Dandelion
Ant	Orange
Fox	Oak tree

PLANTS

HAVE FLOWERS AND SEEDS   HAVE NO FLOWERS AND NO SEEDS   NON-LIVING THINGS

THINGS TO DO

1. Study the animals in a zoo and try to tell what group each animal belongs in.

2. Make a picture zoo. Gather all the pictures of animals that you can find and separate them into groups. Get a scrapbook and paste the pictures in by groups.

3. Find two plants that you can bring to school. Try to get plants that are very different from each other. Be ready to tell everything you can about the structure of each plant. Show how the plants are alike and how they are different.

4. Make these signs and put each one at the top of a large piece of cardboard—Mammals, Birds, Fish, Reptiles, Amphibians, Insects, Plants with Seeds, and Plants without Seeds. Find pictures of animals and plants in magazines. Paste each picture on the correct piece of cardboard. Explain how you decided in which group each plant or animal belongs.

5. Take a walk around the neighborhood. Make a list of all the living things you see. Then separate them into their right groups.

6. Make large charts that tell the important things about each group of animals and plants that you have studied. Put pictures on the charts.

7. If you live near the seashore, make a collection of seaweeds. Find out how to mount them on cards.

8. Find out whether a bat is a mammal or a bird.

9. Read about snakes in books or magazines. Find out how snakes often help people.

10. Find out if a whale is a fish.

★ *In Unit Two You Will Learn* ★

★ *What air is* ★ *Where air is found* ★
★ *What part of the air animals need* ★
★ *How plants get and use air* ★ *Where water is found* ★
★ *Why plants and animals need water* ★

★ UNIT 2 ★

Why Do All Living Things Need Air and Water?

ONE SUMMER John went on an automobile trip with his father and mother. They drove through a part of our country that was very strange to them. For miles and miles there was hardly a living thing. They saw only a few low bushes. Once in a while they saw a bird.

"Why don't more things live here?" John asked.

"Because there isn't enough water," answered his father. "Rain falls only a few times a year, and the sun is so hot that the ground dries up quickly. There are many other places in the world where there is almost no water. These places are called *deserts*. Very few kinds of plants and animals can live in deserts."

John thought that he could understand why living things need water. There was no drinking water in the car and none along the road. He was so thirsty that he could hardly stand it. And he felt as if he were drying up.

If you have some plants and animals at school or at home, you know that water is one of the things they need. Plants and animals need food, too. Every living thing in the world must have water and food.

But water and food are not enough to keep living things alive. Something else is needed. When you are in swimming, can you stay under water very long? Why? What would happen to grasshoppers if you kept them in a small glass jar with the top screwed on tight? You might put in plenty of food and water, but even then they could not live. They must have another very important thing. Do you know what it is? It is air. Every living thing must have air.

47

You could live about three days without water, but you could live only seven minutes without air. Divers who work deep under water and aviators who fly very high above the earth must have special supplies of air.

What is air?

WE CANNOT see air. We cannot smell it, either. And we cannot cut off a piece of air with a knife. Yet air is just as real as anything that you can see and cut. You can prove that air really is something by doing an experiment with a glass.

The glass probably looks empty to you. But is it? If you think it really is empty, do this. Pour three or four inches of water into a deep pan. Put a cork or chip of wood on the water to help you see what happens. Then turn the glass upside down over the cork or chip. Push the glass straight down into the water to the bottom of the pan. Does the water go up into the glass?

Something is keeping the water out of the glass. Tip the glass slowly to one side. Do some big bubbles suddenly come out of the glass and up through the water? Does some water then go into the glass? The bubbles are air. Air has to come out of the glass before water can go in. This

shows you that air takes up room. It takes up room in the same way that rocks and wood and iron take up room.

Even though we cannot cut off a piece of air and wrap it up, still we can fill a paper bag with air. Get a paper bag and blow into it as the boy in the picture is doing. What makes the bag swell out? Feel the bag. Does this show you that air is something?

But air is not like wood, stone, iron, and glass. Wood, stone, iron, and glass are all called *solids*. Solids cannot be poured like water. They keep their shapes. Water is not a solid. Water is a *liquid*. Gasoline, milk, and oil are also liquids.

Air is not a solid, and it is not a liquid. Air is a *gas*. Every material in the world is a solid or a liquid or a gas. Sometimes the same material can be a solid, a liquid, or a gas. Water is a liquid. But when water is frozen into ice, it is changed to a solid. And if water is heated enough, it will change to a gas we call steam.

You have seen many liquids and solids, but did you ever see a gas? Some kinds of gases can be seen easily because they have color. Some are blue, some are yellow, and some are green. Other gases have no color. You can smell some kinds of gases, but some other kinds you cannot smell. Can you smell or see the gas

from a gas stove when you first turn it on?

The air you breathe is not just one kind of gas. It is made up of several different kinds of gases. These gases are all mixed together. So we say that air is a mixture of gases. Some of the gases in air are very important to living things. Let us see what the two most important ones are.

One of the gases in the air is called *oxygen*. No one has ever seen oxygen, because it has no color. No one has ever smelled oxygen, either, because it has no smell. But it is in the air just the same. You will soon learn how very important oxygen is to living things.

There is a much smaller amount of another important gas in the air. It is called *carbon dioxide*. Later, when you study more about plants, you will learn how plants use carbon dioxide. There are several other gases in the air, but you do not need to know about them now.

---

1. *Name three things that plants and animals need to grow and stay alive.*
2. *Tell about two experiments that you can do to show that air really is something even though we cannot see it.*
3. *Name a solid that is in your schoolroom. Is there a liquid in your room? Is there a gas? Can you find something in your room that is not a solid or a liquid or a gas?*
4. *What two important gases are in air?*
5. *How can a liquid such as water be changed to a solid? How can it be changed to a gas? How can a solid be changed to a liquid?*
6. *How can you tell the difference between a solid and a liquid?*

Where is air found?

YOU ARE REALLY living at the bottom of an ocean of air, because the earth is covered with a great layer of air. You walk around on the bottom of this ocean, and you push the air aside as you walk. How high above the earth do you think the air really goes? It goes up more than 500 miles. But most of the air is near the earth. High up above the earth the air is very thin.

You are looking through air when you look at this page. Air is all around you. If you wave a piece of paper in the air, you can feel air pushing against it. There is air in your clothes. Hold up one thickness of cloth very near an electric-light bulb or toward a window. You can see the hundreds of little spaces in the cloth. Air crowds into these spaces. It crowds into every crack and corner of the earth.

You already know that there is air in water. Fish could not live in water if it had no air in it for them to breathe. Plants that grow entirely under the water must have air, too.

You can do an easy experiment that will show you that there is air in water. Heat a pan of water on a stove and watch the water carefully

The frogs must come up to the surface of the water for air.

The diver has air sent down to him through the tubes that lead to his helmet.

while it heats. What do you see on the bottom and sides of the pan as the water heats? These are bubbles of air coming out of the water.

You may be surprised to learn that air is found in still another place. Drop a lump of soil into a glass of water and watch it closely. What do you see coming from the soil? These are bubbles of air.

Earthworms, moles, and other animals that live in the ground must have air to breathe. After a heavy rain, you will often find many earthworms on top of the ground. The rain water has filled up the spaces between the bits of soil. So the earthworms have to come out on top of the ground to get air. As the water sinks down deeper into the soil, the air goes back into the spaces. Then the earthworms go back into the soil.

1. *Name three places where air is found.*
2. *In what ways can you show that there is air in the three places you named?*
3. *Is there any air inside your body? How do you know?*
4. *Why do you have to take deeper breaths of air if you are up on a high mountain?*

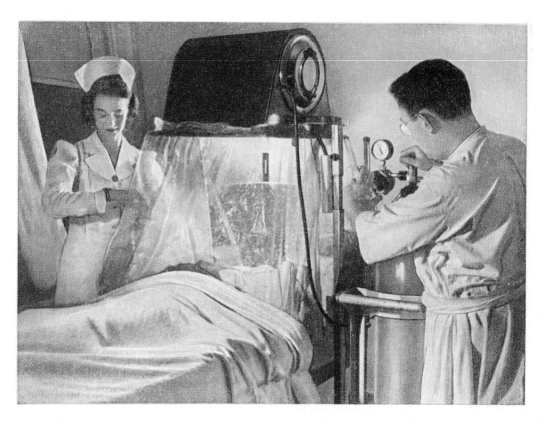

The doctor is giving this girl some oxygen from the large green tank. This will help her breathe more easily.

What part of the air do animals need?

ONCE LONG AGO a scientist was much interested in finding out how living things use air. He had just discovered that air is a mixture of gases. Up to that time everyone thought that air was just one kind of gas. This scientist wanted to know whether animals needed all of the air or just a part of it. Almost everyone knew that living things need air, but they did not know why.

One day the scientist thought of this experiment. He took a glass jar that could be made airtight. Then he caught a mouse and put it inside the glass jar. He closed the jar so tightly that no fresh air could get in. What do you think happened?

At first, the mouse ran around and jumped up the sides of the glass jar. But soon it began to get tired. It moved about more slowly. It did not try to climb the sides of the jar. At last, it seemed to be quite sleepy and did not move around at all.

"Now," the scientist thought, "perhaps the mouse has used up just one kind of gas that is in the air. I'll see if it is the oxygen that the mouse has used. I'll pump some oxygen into the glass jar, and I'll not put in any other gas."

The scientist began to pump oxygen slowly into the jar. What do you think the mouse did? It began to jump and run around again. It acted as lively as when it was first put into the jar. The scientist tried the same experiment with other animals. He found that they could live as long as there was oxygen. When the oxygen was used up, they died if he did not give them more. In this way the scientist found out that animals must have oxygen from the air if they are to stay alive.

Right now, as you read this, you are breathing. Have you ever stopped to think that you breathe air all day long and all night long? When you breathe, oxygen along with the other gases in the air goes into your lungs. When the mixture is breathed out again, some of the oxygen is left inside your body. What do you think the oxygen does for you? Why must you have oxygen to live?

To keep alive, your body must be warm. The heat to keep you warm is made when the food you eat and the oxygen you breathe join in your body. Oxygen joins with food in your muscles. This must happen before your muscles can make your body move. Not one part of your body could move without oxygen. Even your heart would stop beating. Now do you understand why you must always have a good supply of the oxygen that is in the air?

---

1. *What was the scientist trying to find out about air and living things?*
2. *What did the scientist do to find out whether oxygen was a part of the air needed by animals?*
3. *What did scientists have to discover before they could find out how living things use air?*
4. *Why should we sometimes change the water in a fish bowl?*
5. *Does the air you breathe out have as much oxygen in it as the air you breathe in?*
6. *Why do animals need oxygen?*

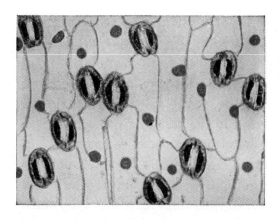

If you could look at a leaf with a microscope, you would see the tiny openings.

The floating leaves of water lilies have openings only on their upper sides.

How do plants get and use air?

PLANTS, TOO, need air. Do you know how they get it? If you could look at the upper and lower sides of a leaf with a microscope, you would find many tiny openings. In most plants there are more of them on the underside of the leaf than there are on the upper side. Now let us find out just how important these little openings are to plants.

Get two small potted plants of the same kind. Spread some vaseline on both the upper and the lower sides of all the leaves of one of the plants. This will fill up the openings. Watch the plants and see what happens. It may be some time before any change takes place. Do the leaves get yellow and drop off the plant that has the vaseline on its leaves? Does this plant finally die? Do you know why?

Air goes into the leaves through these openings. If these openings are filled up, the plant cannot get air. And if it does not get air, it dies. Plants must have air just as animals must have air.

In summer, the openings in leaves of plants along the side of a dusty road sometimes get filled up with dust. In cities, where dirt and dust from many factories cover the leaves, it is very hard to grow plants. The dust and dirt fill the tiny openings in the leaf and keep out the air. Of course, if a plant cannot breathe, it will soon die. That is why people sometimes put some of the house plants in the sink or bathtub and wash their leaves.

Now let us see what plants do with the air that goes in through the tiny

The roots of plants must have air, too. This beautiful elm tree died because so much heavy soil was put over the roots. The roots could not get enough air.

openings in the leaves. Plants need the oxygen in the air that they take in just as animals do. As you know, plants must have food to stay alive and grow. Without oxygen, plants cannot use food.

But there is another gas in the air that green plants must have. This gas is carbon dioxide. Plants use carbon dioxide to make food. Animals do not make their own food, but green plants do. Later in your study of science, you will learn more about how green plants use carbon dioxide from the air to make food. So you see that green plants need two gases that are in the air. These gases are oxygen and carbon dioxide.

1. *In the experiment, the leaves of one plant were covered with vaseline. No vaseline was put on the leaves of the other plant. Why were two plants used in the experiment?*
2. *Can you find anything in this list of things that does not need oxygen?*
   Cat   Tree   Stone   Insect   Fish   Dead tree   Bird
3. *Why do plants need oxygen? Why do they need carbon dioxide?*

Most maps cannot show all the ponds, rivers, and lakes. But you could see how many there are if you could look down on the earth from an airplane.

Where is water found?

THERE WAS PLENTY of air in the desert that John and his father and mother saw on their automobile trip. Plants could get all the oxygen and carbon dioxide they needed. Animals had plenty of oxygen. Yet very few plants and animals could live in the desert where there was only a little water.

Every living thing must have water. So it is a good thing that water is found almost everywhere on earth. The water in oceans, seas, lakes, and rivers covers about three fourths of all the earth. Get a map of the world and look at the places that are colored blue. They are the oceans, lakes, and seas. You can see that they cover much more of the earth than the land does.

But not all of the water is in oceans, seas, lakes, and rivers. Some of it is in the ground. When it rains, much water soaks down into the earth. We use this water that soaks down into the earth. We dig wells and put pipes down into the earth so that we can pump the water up.

This story tells you another place where water is found.

Jane's mother had promised to take her to the park for a picnic with her friends. On the day of the picnic Jane said, "Oh, Mother! It rained last night. The grass and trees are very wet. We can't have our picnic."

But Jane's mother looked at the sky and said, "All the clouds have gone, and the sun is shining. By afternoon the leaves of the trees, the grass, and even the swings in the park will all be dry."

When it was time for the picnic, Jane found that her mother was right. Do you know where the water had gone? Where does the water go when the wet clothes on the clothesline dry? You can tell if you do this experiment.

Pour water into a glass. Put a rubber band or a string around the glass. Have it even with the top of the water to show just how much water there is in the glass. Make a sign saying "Please do not touch," and set it by the glass. Look at the water in the glass every day. What is happening to the water? Where do you think the water is going?

Does all the water in the glass finally disappear? When water slowly disappears into the air, we say that it *evaporates*. The water changes from a liquid to a gas and mixes with the other gases in the air. When water has turned into a gas in this way, we call it *water vapor*.

Water is always evaporating from places on the earth. Water evaporates from wet ground and from wet trees. Water is always going into the air from lakes, oceans, rivers, and creeks.

There is always some water vapor in the air. There really is water vapor between your eyes and the page of this book. But you cannot see the water vapor.

Perhaps you are wondering whether this water ever gets out of the air again. Here is an easy way to find out. First, be sure that your hands are dry. Then take a dry metal cup and fill it with very cold water or ice that has been chopped into small pieces. Stir the ice and watch the outside of the tin cup. What do you see on the outside of the cup? Where does this water come from?

Can it come from the inside of the cup? Why?

If you used a good metal cup, there were no holes in it. So the water from the melted ice could not get through to the outside. If your hands were dry, the water could not have come from them. There is only one place where the water could have come from. It had to come from the air around the outside of the cup. Let us see why this happens.

Cold air can hold less water than warm air. The ice in the cup made the cup cold. The air that touched the outside of the cup became cooler. Some of the water vapor in the air changed to a liquid and came out of the air. Little drops of water gathered on the outside of the cup. We say that the water vapor *condensed* on the cup. Condense means change from a gas to a liquid.

Have you ever watched water come out of the air? Of course you have. Rain is water condensed from the water vapor in the air. Hail and sleet are frozen rain. Snow comes from water vapor that has frozen in the air. Dew and frost also come from water vapor in the air. Rain, hail, sleet, snow, dew, and frost all come from condensed water vapor.

Water is always going into the air from the lakes, rivers, oceans, ponds, and puddles. Can you imagine what would happen if this water could not come out of the air again? We would soon have no more water on the earth. We have plenty of water because the water vapor in the air can condense to make rain or snow.

1. *What are the missing words in the statements below?*
    a) *When water goes into the air, we say it ____.*
    b) *Water changes to ____ ____ when it goes into the air.*
    c) *When water vapor comes out of the air, we say it ____.*
2. *Where is water found? Write your answer to this question and read it to the class.*
3. *Should you heat air or cool it to make the water vapor in it condense? How do you know?*
4. *What happens on the outside of a pitcher of ice water or ice-cold lemonade when it is brought into a room on a hot summer day? Why does this happen?*
5. *A boy wearing eyeglasses on a cold winter day came into a warm room. His glasses clouded up so that he could not see through them. Why did this happen?*

In parts of our country where there is not much rain, trees can grow only along the banks of streams. The next three pages will help you understand why this is true.

Why must plants have water?

Do you know why plants must have water? There is something very wonderful that water and other liquids can do. Let us find out what it is. Then we can understand why plants need water.

Suppose someone asked you to pass some sugar through a cloth without tearing the cloth. How would you do it? Perhaps you think you could not do it, but try this experiment. Drop some sugar into a glass of water. Stir the water until you can no longer see the sugar. Taste the water. Where is the sugar?

The sugar is in the water. Scientists say that the water *dissolves* the sugar. Water is the world's best dissolver. It can dissolve more things than any other liquid can. Now pour the water through the cloth. Taste the water again. Did the sugar go through the cloth?

When the sugar is dissolved, it can pass through the cloth. You can do the same thing with some salt. Try it and see if this is true.

Now let us see how water helps plants because it can dissolve so many materials.

Perhaps you have watched someone spread *fertilizer* on a lawn. The fertilizer is made up of materials that the grass needs for making food. But if it is left on top of the ground, the fertilizer does not help the grass grow. So the person who is spreading the fertilizer, waters the lawn. Or he waits for the rain to fall.

The water that falls on the lawn dissolves the fertilizer. Then the water with the dissolved fertilizer soaks into the ground. When it soaks down where the roots of the grass are, the roots begin to take in the water. The dissolved fertilizer goes into the roots with the water.

Now you can understand why plants need water. The materials that plants need to make food are in the soil. But these materials have to be dissolved in water before they can

soak into the plant roots. Plants could never get the materials from the soil if the water did not bring them in. Plants could not live in the best soil in the world if they did not have water.

Let us see if we can find another way in which water helps plants. Put some red ink in a glass of water. Then put a stalk of celery that has some leaves on it into the red water. Watch the celery for a while. How long does it take the red water to go up the stalk and into the leaves?

Water is the world's best dissolver. It is also one of the best carriers. It can go from one place to another very easily. As it moves, it carries along the materials that are dissolved in it. The water with the dissolved materials in it soaks into the roots of a plant. Then it travels up the stem to the leaves of the plant. This watery liquid that travels through the plant is called *sap*.

Here is an easy experiment to show you that plants need water to grow. Get a yard or more of white cloth. Fold it several times until it is about the size of a handkerchief. Now sprinkle the cloth with water until it is quite damp. Lay about two dozen bean seeds on the cloth. Then roll it up with the seeds inside. Sprinkle the cloth with water every day so that it will not dry out.

Take another cloth of the same size. Fold it and lay the same number of bean seeds on it. Roll this cloth up just as you did the other one. Do not wet this cloth. Keep both cloths in the same place for a week. Then open them up and look at the seeds. What do you find? Why did something happen to one set of seeds that did not happen to the other set?

The bean seeds have baby plants inside them. The seeds also have food inside them for these tiny plants to use for growing. But the tiny plants cannot use this hard food unless they have water to change and dissolve it. The baby plants in the seeds that were rolled up in the dry cloth could not use the hard food that was around them. But the water from the wet cloth around the other seeds changed and dissolved the food so that the plants could use it for growing. Does this experiment show you why plants need water to grow even when they are inside a seed?

---

1. *Water helps plants in two important ways. What are they?*
2. *How does water help seeds start growing? How could you show that seeds need water to start growing?*
3. *Choose the right word for this sentence. Water (evaporates—dissolves—condenses) food for the plant. How do you know that you are right?*
4. *Suppose nothing in the world would dissolve. Would that make any difference to you? Explain your answer.*
5. *Why are rains in the spring very important?*
6. *Write five things you have learned about water and plants.*
7. *Why do you think the trees in the picture on page 59 are growing only along the river banks?*

These animals live in a very dry part of Africa where there is not much water except in small pools or water holes.

Why do animals need water?

ALMOST EVERY KIND of animal in the world must have water just about every day. You could live for a month without food, but you would die in about three days without water. Nearly three fourths of your body is made up of water. If you stopped drinking water long enough, your body would dry up like the leaves and the grass in the hot summer months.

Why do we and other living things need water for our bodies? Water helps our bodies use food. The food we eat has to be dissolved before our bodies can use it. The water we drink helps dissolve the food we eat. You would have a hard time swallowing dry cookies and bread if the *saliva* in your mouth did not moisten them for you. Saliva is one of the body's juices. It is made partly of water.

There are many juices in your body that keep food moist and dissolve it. Your body cannot use dry food any more than a baby plant can use the dry food in a seed. Without water, your body could not make these juices that change food so that we can use it. In the next unit you will learn more about this.

All animals must have water. So many different kinds of animals can often be found around one water hole at the same time.

The blood of animals is made up mostly of water. If animals did not have water to drink, they would not have blood to keep them alive. The blood in your body acts in much the same way that sap in a plant does. It carries food and oxygen around inside your body.

When you eat food, all you need to do is to chew it and swallow it. Then it goes down into your stomach. But it has to go down to your toes and up to your arms and head. Every part of your body needs some of the food. Your blood carries the food to all parts of your body. It carries oxygen, too. Both food and oxygen must be carried to the places in the body where the food is used. Do you see now why someone once said, "Without water, nothing could stay alive on the earth"?

1. *Make a list of the things you have learned about animals and water.*
2. *Why must your body have water to use food?*
3. *When you are thirsty, how does your mouth feel?*

Can you tell where the frost on the window came from?

QUESTIONS TO ANSWER

1. Why does a person die if he stays under water too long?

2. When aviators fly high above the earth, they need a special supply of oxygen. What does this tell you about the air high above the earth?

3. Which gas in the air helps living things use food? Which gas helps green plants make food?

4. Sometimes hot water looks milky when it comes from the faucet. Can you think of a reason for this?

5. Where does the drinking water in your home come from?

6. About how many glasses of water do you drink in a day? Why is it important for you to drink plenty of water?

7. How does a plant look when it does not have enough water?

8. What happens to a farmer's crops if there is no rain for a long time?

9. Why should you hang up wet clothes if you want them to dry?

10. Why do clothes dry more quickly on a windy day than on a day when there is no wind?

1. Find out how fresh air is kept coming into your schoolroom.

2. Show your class that

a) There is air in a glass bottle.

b) A solid can be changed to a liquid.

c) A liquid can be changed to a gas.

d) A liquid can be changed to a solid.

3. Learn more about how deep-sea divers get air.

4. Cut open the stalk of celery that you put in red ink and find the parts that are colored. These colored parts carry the water to the leaves.

5. Dig up a dandelion plant and look at the roots. Dig up some grass and look at the roots. Does the dandelion plant have longer roots than the grass? Why can a dandelion plant stay green longer than grass in the dry summer months?

6. Find some green leaves and look for the parts of the leaves that carry water.

7. Find out if there is much water in a peach or in an apple. First, weigh one of these fruits. Heat it for a long time in an oven. Then weigh it again. The heat made the water evaporate from the fruit. Was there much water in the fruit?

8. Find out more about how desert plants can live where there is so little water.

9. Make a list of the new science words you learned in this unit and show the class that you know what each word means.

10. Find out more about oxygen, carbon dioxide, and other gases in air.

★ In Unit Three You Will Learn ★

★ How your body is like a machine ★ How your bones help you ★ How your body can move ★ How your body uses the food you eat ★ How food is carried to all parts of your body ★ How your body gets oxygen ★ What skin does for your body ★ How you know what goes on around you ★ What keeps the parts of your body working together ★

★ UNIT 3 ★

How Does Your Body Work?

WHEN THE BOYS and girls of a science class came into the room one day, they found these sentences on the blackboard.

I am the best machine in the world.

I can lift things.

I can remember things I do.

I can change a glass of milk into part of me.

I can tell if anything comes near me.

I need something to make me go, and I can get it myself.

I can run myself.

I can repair myself.

There are millions of machines like me.

What am I?

It took the boys and girls a few minutes to guess the right answer. Bobby said, "It's not an automobile, because an automobile can't lift things, and it can't repair itself, and it can't tell when anything comes near it."

Henry said, "I never saw a machine that could run itself and repair itself."

Then the teacher smiled and said, "There are thirty of these machines in this room now. They are all running. They can all do the things told in the sentences on the board."

Quickly Helen spoke up, "You mean the boys and girls! We are the machines that can do all of these things."

How is your body like a machine?

THE ENGINE OF YOUR father's automobile is a machine. It is made of many different parts. There are big parts and little parts. There are parts that move and parts that do not move. All the parts work together to make

the engine run. Your body, too, is made of many parts that work together so that you can do what you want to do. In this way your body is like a machine.

All human machines have parts that are alike. These parts are made up of hundreds of smaller parts. There is the main part of your body called the *trunk*. You have other parts called arms, legs, and head. Inside your head and trunk there are dozens of other parts.

An automobile engine will run if it is supplied with gasoline. Of course, you do not need gasoline to make you move. But you do need food. You have a stomach that needs food three times a day so that you will have strength to move. Your body uses this food very much as the engine uses gasoline. To keep going, both you and the engine must be fed.

To keep going, an engine must be kept in good repair. Its parts must be oiled. Broken parts must be repaired or replaced. If any part does not do its work, the engine will not run properly. Your parts must be kept in good working order, too. A stomach ache, a headache, or a broken bone will keep you from doing your best work. Both your body and the engine must be kept in good condition.

So you see that your body and its parts are in many ways like the engine that runs the automobile. But your body can do many things that an automobile engine cannot do. There is no machine on earth so wonderful as a human body.

Did you ever try to count the different things your body does? Try to remember what it has done since you got out of bed this morning. One part of your body did some work that made you *hear* your mother call you. Many parts of your body worked together so that you could *dress* yourself and *wash* your hands and face. You *felt* your shoes to see whether they were still wet from the day before. Just as you finished washing, you *smelled* some of the good food that your mother was cooking for your breakfast. You *ran* downstairs to eat.

All this time you were using your eyes. You *saw* the sun and all the things around you. You *knew* that this would be a good day for the hike you had planned to take after school.

You *tasted* the food you ate for breakfast. You *remembered* to ask your father if you could use his pocketknife. When he answered, you knew what he said.

Count up the different things your body did. You heard sounds, dressed yourself and washed, felt your shoes, smelled food, ran, saw many things, and tasted food. You listened, and you talked. You remembered, and you knew what people were talking about. All of these things you did before you had been out of bed an hour. Can you think of any machine that can do so many different things?

---

1. *What does your body use to make it go?*
2. *Why should you know some of the important things about your body?*
3. *Why should you take care of your body even more carefully than of an expensive machine?*
4. *How is your body like a machine? How is it different from a machine?*

How do your bones help you?

DID YOU EVER SEE or hear of an animal called a *jellyfish?* Just from the name, what do you think a jellyfish looks like? You can probably guess. It is just like a mass of jelly floating in the water. It has no bones in its body. Your body would be almost like that if you did not have a framework of bones to hold up the soft flesh. As you know, this framework is called a skeleton.

You have seen many kinds of bones—chicken bones, fish bones, turkey bones, pig bones, and cow bones. Perhaps when you were out in the woods or fields, you found the skeleton of some animal that had died.

You need a framework just as an umbrella needs its steel ribs and its

handle and just as a house needs rafters and beams. The bones of the skeleton make up the framework of your body. How many bones do you think there are in your skeleton? There are over 200! Now let us see what this framework of yours is like.

It is made of long bones and short bones, flat bones and round bones. Some of them are broad and flat. Others are long and narrow. Many are very small. Can you feel some of these bones in your fingers, arms, and legs? All of these bones are part of your skeleton.

Look at the picture on page 71 and find the long row of bones along the back of the skeleton. These bones make up what is called the *backbone,* or *spine.* Your backbone or spine holds your body up just as a pole holds up a tent. But your backbone is also made so that you can bend it.

Someone once said that this backbone is like many spools put together on a string. You can see in the picture that it is made up of many small bones. Press your fingers tightly against your backbone. Can you feel the places where the bones come together? Each one of these little bones has a hole through it. These holes make a long, hollow tube through the whole length of the backbone. A white cord, called the *spinal cord*, fills this tube. Later in this unit, you will find out what the spinal cord does.

Between each two bones of your spine there is a soft cushion that acts like a pad. This little cushion keeps the bones from grinding against each other when they move. The cushions are made of *cartilage*. Your ears and nose have cartilage in them, too. When we find cartilage in meat, we call it *gristle*. Tough cords that are called *ligaments* hold the bones of your spine and other parts of your body together. Do you see now why you can bend your back so easily?

Your backbone is a very important part of your skeleton. It helps hold the rest of your body framework together. It is somewhat like the frame of a bicycle to which the wheels, pedals, and handlebars are attached. Your head, arms, legs, and ribs are attached either to your backbone or to other bones that are attached to your backbone.

Look at the picture on page 72. Do these animal skeletons have backbones, too? Mammals, birds, reptiles, amphibians, and fish are all animals that have backbones.

Bones do more than just support your body and give it shape. You can see what else bones do if you feel the top and sides of your head. Inside your head you have a very tender

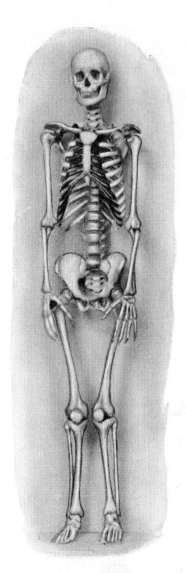

brain. Your brain is protected on the outside by a boxlike covering of bones called the *skull*. Sometimes boys find skulls of rabbits or other animals in the woods and bring them to school. It is easy to see that these skulls made a strong cover to protect the brains that once were inside them. Find the skull in the picture of the

Here are the skeletons of some animals. Can you tell what kinds of animals they are from the shapes of their skeletons?

skeleton on page 71. Look at the skeletons of the animals on this page. Do they have skulls, too?

Feel your ribs. Can you feel how close together they are? Perhaps you can count them. There are twelve ribs on each side. Look at the picture on page 71. Can you see how the ribs make a cage that helps keep the heart and lungs from being hurt?

---

1. *Describe the structure of your skeleton.*
2. *What does your backbone do for you?*
3. *How is your spine made so that it can bend easily?*
4. *How do your bones protect you?*
5. *Write down what you have learned about each of these.*
     Skull   Skeleton   Cartilage   Ligaments   Backbone
   Read to the class what you have written.

How can your body move?

THE BOYS AND GIRLS in the science class were getting ready for a marionette show. Betty was making a marionette farmer. It was the first time she had ever tried to make one. "My Farmer Jim is finished," she said. "But I don't think he will ever move. He is so very stiff."

"You must make joints in his arms and legs so that the parts of his body can move," said the teacher. "You have made his body all in one piece. I'll help you make the joints. Then we will fasten strings to every part of his body that we want to move. I think you will be able to make Farmer Jim walk, run, and even load hay into a wagon if you can work the strings well enough."

Your skeleton would be about as useless as Betty's marionette if all your bones were joined solidly together like the legs, arms, and back of a chair. Of course, the bones must be held together. But most bones must be free to move.

On the next page, are pictures of the bones in the arm and the leg. Find the elbow. Your elbow is the place where the two big bones in your arm are joined together. We call a place like this, a *joint*.

The bones are held together at the joint by ligaments. These ligaments

let the bones move, and at the same time they keep the bones from coming apart. Look carefully at the picture of the arm bones. Then try to feel the bones in your own arm. Bend your arm and feel the bones and the joint.

There are joints in your body at every place where the bones can move. You can bend your legs and

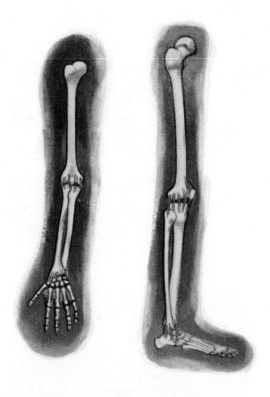

toes when you walk because there are joints in both your legs and your toes. Where are the joints that make it possible for you to play a piano or to hold a pencil? Look at the pic-

ture of the skeleton on page 71 and find the places where there are joints.

The joints were not able to make Betty's marionette move. You remember how she made it move. To move its arms, she fastened strings to the arms. When she pulled the strings, the arms moved. To move its legs, she fastened strings to them, too. The head could not move, either, until it had a string to move it.

The strings that Betty tied to the parts of her marionette acted much as the movers of your body do. On the next page is a picture that shows the *muscles* of a body. Your muscles are the movers of your body. You can see that there are muscles fastened to the bones. They are fastened so that when the muscles move, the bones must move, too.

An easy way to see how muscles work is to watch them in your arm as you lift a book. Roll your sleeve

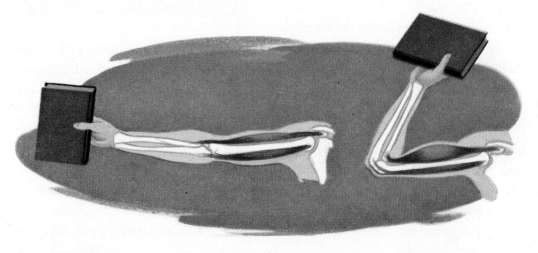

up as far as you can. Pick up a heavy book and lift it slowly toward your face. Watch the big muscle in the upper part of your arm. What happens to it when you lift the book? Do you notice that it gets thicker and shorter? Now watch the muscle as you slowly lay the book back on the table. See it get thinner and longer.

If you feel the under part of your arm, you find that there is another muscle there. Look at the picture and find the muscles. In the picture the muscle on top is colored blue. When the muscle on top pulls to lift a book, the muscle gets short and thick. At the same time the muscle on the underside of your arm gets long and thin. When you pull your arm back, the muscle on the underside gets shorter and thicker. The one on the upper side gets longer and thinner.

If you had a muscle only on top of your arm and none on the underside, you could raise your arm. But you could not pull it back. Most muscles work in pairs like the ones in your arm. Now you can see how muscles work to move parts of your body.

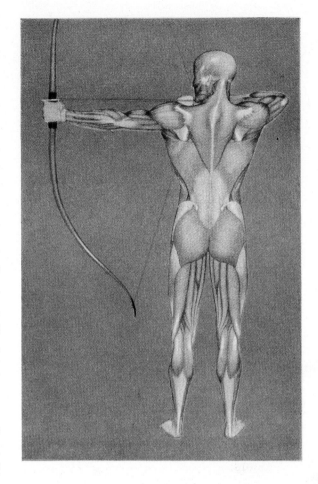

The picture above shows the muscles of a man. Can you see which muscles he is using? What changes in the shape of these muscles are taking place?

1. *Why do you need joints in your body?*
2. *Where are the joints that move when you do these things?*
    Run   Chew   Swim   Write   Talk   Ride a bicycle
3. *How does a muscle change as it pulls on a bone?*
4. *Why are the muscles that move bones usually in pairs?*

How does your body use the food you eat?

DO YOU EVER wonder what happens to the food you eat when it gets inside your body? After you eat a meal, many things happen inside of you that you do not even know about. Your body changes your food so much that you would never guess that it once had been fruit, bread, meat, or milk.

You know, of course, that you are growing. Every part of your body is getting larger. To grow, you have to make the food into part of yourself. If you should break your arm, some of the food would help repair the broken bone. Some of your food gives you the strength to walk to school. In Unit Two you learned that some of the food you eat keeps your body warm, no matter how cold it is outdoors.

Before food can be used in any of these ways, it must be changed to a liquid. We say that food that has been changed to a liquid has been *digested*. Let us see just how your food is digested after you eat it.

First, you put your food into a kind of chopping box. Probably you have never thought of your mouth as a chopping box. But it really is. There are two rows of white choppers in this box. They are your teeth. And your teeth begin to work on your food as soon as you put it into your mouth. They break up your food and chew it into small bits.

Your front teeth are cutters. They have sharp cutting edges such as a hatchet has. They bite into a piece of toast or meat and cut it into smaller bits. Next to these cutters are some teeth that have sharp points. They help cut and tear the food into pieces. Toward the back of your mouth are some teeth with flat tops. These are the grinders. They grind the food into still smaller bits.

Look at the picture. Find the different kinds of teeth in the mouth shown there. Then try to find them in your own mouth. You will not find all of the large grinding teeth. Some of these will not grow in until you are older.

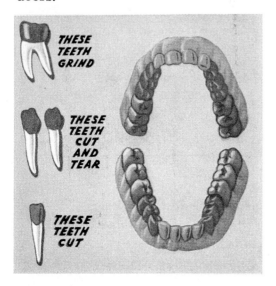

THESE TEETH GRIND

THESE TEETH CUT AND TEAR

THESE TEETH CUT

Did you ever notice that a liquid begins to flow in your mouth when you put food in it? Sometimes this liquid will pour into your mouth when you just see and smell something good to eat. Perhaps you have heard someone say, "That makes my mouth water." As you have learned, this liquid, or juice, is called saliva. It wets the food and makes it easy to swallow. Saliva also helps digest some of the food so that your body can use it.

The food you swallow goes down a tube into your stomach. This tube is about ten inches long and about an inch across. It goes down through your neck and joins the back of your mouth with your stomach.

Look at the picture as you are reading this page. You will see the parts of your body that digest your food, and you can follow the food through the different parts.

When food gets into your stomach, it is ready for about an hour of mixing. You can think of your stomach as a mixing bowl. The walls of this mixing bowl are full of muscles that move the walls back and forth. They squeeze the food and push it from one side to another. These walls also pour a kind of juice on the food. After a time most of the food has been changed into a liquid. Then it is ready to leave your stomach.

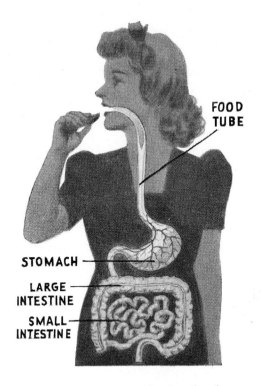

FOOD TUBE

STOMACH

LARGE INTESTINE

SMALL INTESTINE

From your stomach the food goes down into a long tube called the *small intestine*. The small intestine is about twenty feet long and an inch across. It folds together in somewhat the way that a fire hose is folded. The walls of this long tube pour more juices on the food. All these juices help change more and more of the food into a liquid. Then the digested food is ready to pass through the walls of the small intestine into all the other parts of your body.

Not all the food you eat can be changed to a liquid that can pass through the walls of the small intestine. The part of the food that is not digested goes into another tube called the *large intestine*. From the large intestine it is passed out of the body.

It is very important to keep the parts of your body that digest your food in good working condition. Later in your science study you will learn how eating the proper foods helps you do this.

---

1. *Food helps you in four ways. What are they?*
2. *How do you know that food is changed into you?*
3. *What do your teeth do to food?*
4. *Crackers are a very dry food. How can you swallow them?*
5. *How do muscles and juices help us digest the food we eat?*
6. *In Unit Two you learned that your body needs water. How has that helped you understand what you have just read?*
7. *What happens to a piece of bread after you put it into your mouth?*

How is food carried to all parts of your body?

FOOD CANNOT HELP you grow or do you one bit of good if it stays in your small intestine. It is like the food in the grocery store near your home. As long as the food stays in the store, you cannot use it. It must be brought to your home first.

Every part of your body needs food. Your head needs some of it, and so do your feet. Some of the food must be taken to your arms, to your fingers, to all of your muscles, and to your brain. How do you think this food gets from the small intestine to the other parts of your body?

Something must carry the food around in your body. This carrier is your blood. Look at the picture on page 79. This picture shows the wonderful network of tubes, or *blood vessels*, that reaches every part of the body. Look at the picture again and find the heart. This is the pump that keeps the blood moving around through the tubes. Put your hand over your heart. Can you feel your heart beat? It is pumping blood.

Your heart is really a big muscle that is hollow. Blood flows into this hollow muscle from some of the blood vessels. When your heart is full of blood, the muscle squeezes the blood out through other blood vessels. In a moment it fills with blood again. Another squeeze, and out goes the blood. This pumping keeps the blood flowing through the blood vessels day and night.

Look at the picture again. Do you see that the blood vessel which carries the blood away from the heart is very large? Small branches come out from this large vessel somewhat like the branches on a tree. These branches divide into still smaller branches. At last, they get so small that they carry blood into even the smallest part of you. The picture does not show all the small vessels.

As this stream of blood flows through your body, it leaves some of the food it is carrying. It leaves food in all parts of your body, just as a grocery truck might leave food at your door and at the doors of all your neighbors.

Of course, the blood would soon deliver all the food it holds unless it could get a new supply. Some of the blood that flows out of your heart is carried to the small intestine. There are thousands of tiny blood vessels in the walls of the small intestine. The food in the intestine is a liquid that can pass through the walls of the intestine into these tiny blood vessels. When the food gets into the blood, away it goes to all parts of your body. Now you see how the blood gets a new supply of food.

Before the new supply of food can be sent out to the rest of your body, the blood must go to your heart. The tiny blood vessels in the walls of the

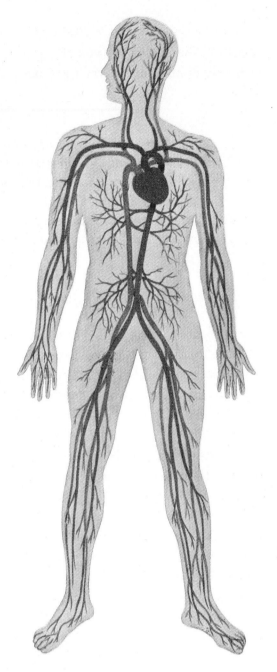

The vessels that are colored red take the blood away from the heart. The ones that are colored blue take the blood back to the heart again.

small intestine join to make larger vessels. These larger vessels join with others that are carrying blood back to your heart. Then your heart pumps the blood to all parts of your body.

---

1. Why must food be carried to all parts of your body?
2. Why must food be digested before it can get into the blood?
3. How do the big blood vessels that leave the heart carry blood to all parts of your body?
4. How is blood kept moving through your body?
5. How are the blood vessels like the branches on a tree?

How do all parts of your body get oxygen?

YOU KNOW THAT you could not live for more than seven minutes if you stopped breathing. And you have learned that your body must have oxygen to use the food that you eat. You know that the oxygen you need comes from the air. You cannot move without oxygen, and you cannot grow without it. Oxygen, like food, is needed by every part of your body. It must be carried by the blood, too.

You already know how you get air into your body. Air comes in when you breathe. Suppose you take a deep breath and see what happens. Do you feel your ribs move out? As they do, air from the outside rushes in through your nose or mouth and fills your lungs. Now breathe out. You can feel your ribs move back in again.

As they do, air is pushed out of your lungs through your nose or mouth.

Now look at the picture on page 81. Air gets into your body through your nose or mouth. Then the air goes into your *windpipe*. The windpipe goes down through your neck. Then it branches into two large tubes. You have two lungs, and one branch of the windpipe goes to each lung.

Your lungs are somewhat like two big sponges with hundreds of tiny pockets in them. After the windpipe branches into two large tubes, each of these parts keeps branching into smaller and smaller tubes. Every one of the tiny branches ends in one of the small pockets in your lungs. These little pockets are filled with air when you breathe in. From there the oxygen gets into your blood.

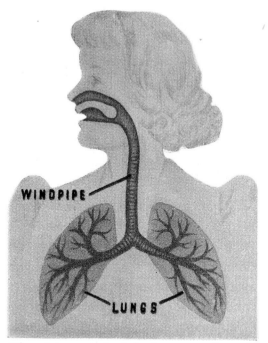
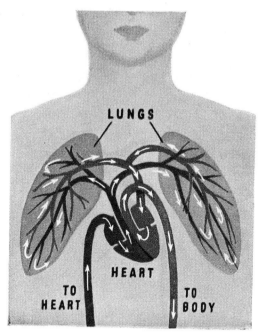

The picture at the left shows you how the air you breathe in gets to your lungs. Look at the picture on the right and follow the white arrows. You will see how your blood gets from your heart to your lungs and back again with a new supply of oxygen.

Now let us see how the oxygen gets from the air in these pockets into your blood. During its journey around your body, all of your blood goes through your lungs. The blood vessels separate into tiny tubes in the lungs. The walls of every air pocket are full of these tiny blood tubes.

The walls of the air pockets and the walls of the blood tubes are very thin.

So the oxygen passes easily from the air pockets into the blood in the tiny blood tubes. When the oxygen gets into your blood, it is carried everywhere your blood goes. It is unloaded all through your body while the food is being unloaded. The blood that has unloaded its oxygen goes back to your heart. Then it goes to your lungs for a new supply of oxygen.

1. *Where does the air go when you breathe it in through your nose or mouth?*
2. *Where does the blood get the oxygen to carry through your body?*
3. *How is the way that the blood gets oxygen like the way that the blood gets food?*

What does your skin do for your body?

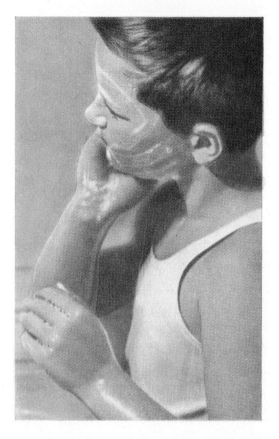

YOUR CLOTHES may get soaked in a heavy rain, but none of the water gets inside your body. Your body has a covering that keeps the water out. This covering is the skin. It covers all the parts of your body, from head to toe.

But keeping water out of your body is not the only thing your skin does. Your skin also keeps out dirt. Even more important, your skin keeps out *germs*. Germs are very tiny plants or animals that can make you sick when they get inside your body. Most germs cannot go through your skin unless the skin is cut or burned. A cut or a burn in the skin is an open door for germs that can make you sick. That is why you must always take care of a cut or a burn and keep your skin clean. Washing your face with soap and warm water helps keep the germs off.

If you could look at your skin through a magnifying glass, you would find hundreds of tiny openings. These small openings, or *pores*, let the *perspiration* come out of your body. Perspiration is a liquid. It is mostly water. But it also has in it materials that your body needs to get rid of. These waste materials are formed when food is used by your body. Some of these waste materials come out of the body in perspiration.

---

1. *In what three ways does your skin help you?*
2. *Tell what you have learned about germs.*
3. *Why should you wash yourself with soap and warm water?*

How do you know what goes on around you?

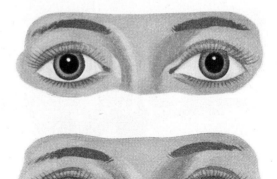

DO YOU EVER PLAY "blindman's buff"? If you are the "blindman," you have something tied over your eyes so that you cannot see. Your friends are in a circle around you. One of them comes inside the circle. And you try to catch him and guess who he is. You listen carefully, and you hear him behind you. You turn around, but he has moved. Then you hear him on the other side. You run after him.

In a few minutes you catch him. You feel his jacket, and you can tell by feeling it that it is made of leather. John is the only one who has a leather jacket on. So you know it must be John. Your *sense of hearing* and your *sense of touch* have helped you catch John and tell who he is.

There are five senses that help you. They are very important to you because they tell you what is going on around you. Let us see what these five senses are. Suppose you look at your eyes in a mirror. Do you see the very dark place in the center of each eye? This dark spot is the *pupil* of the eye. The pupils are like windows in your eyes. They let in the light. If these pupils did not let in the light, you could not see what is going on around you. You would not have any *sense of sight*.

If there is too much light coming into your eyes, the pupils have a way of shutting out some of the light. Very tiny muscles in your eyes make the pupils larger or smaller. On very bright days, or if you are reading in bright light, the muscles close the pupils part way so that less light comes in. At night, or when you are in a dark place, the muscles open the pupils of your eyes wider to let in more light. In the picture, which eyes are in a bright light?

Have you ever gone from the bright outdoors into a dark room? Do you remember how dark it seemed at first? Then you began to see things. In a few minutes you could see fairly well. The muscles in your eyes needed time to open the pupils wider to let in more light. Inside the dark room there was not much light. So the pupils needed to be open wide.

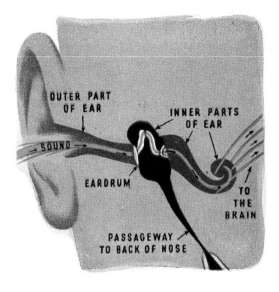

OUTER PART OF EAR

INNER PARTS OF EAR

SOUND

EARDRUM

TO THE BRAIN

PASSAGEWAY TO BACK OF NOSE

The outside of your ear catches these sounds. Then they travel to the inside of your ear. You can hear sounds coming from all directions. When a sound comes from one side of you, you hear it louder in one ear than in the other. This is how you can tell the direction of a sound. The picture shows you what your ear looks like and the path that sounds follow through it.

Sometimes you can tell what is cooking on the stove without going into the kitchen. You do not see or hear what is cooking, but you know what it is. Of course, you know how you can tell. You smell it. You are using your *sense of smell*. Some of the smell of the cooking food comes out into the air in the room. You breathe the air through your nose, and then you know what you are going to have for dinner.

Let us suppose that you are blindfolded. You also are holding your nose so that no air can get in. Now someone puts a piece of candy in your mouth. You cannot see it, and you cannot smell it. How can you tell what it is? You use your *sense of taste*. In your mouth are tiny parts, or *tasters*, that tell you things about anything you put in your mouth. If you did not have these, a piece of candy and a pickle would be the same to you because you could not taste either one.

Your eyes tell you what is going on around you. You can see things that are very close to you, and you can see things that are very far away. Your eyes tell you how large or small a thing is. They tell you its color. If you had no eyes, it would be like living in a dark closet all the time.

Your ears give you the *sense of hearing*. They are your sound catchers. They can catch the sound of the wind whispering through the trees, and they can catch the sound of a great explosion. They catch hundreds of different sounds every hour. Without these very important sound catchers, you could never hear what people tell you. They would talk to you, and you would only see their lips move. Think of the interesting and important things you would miss if you could not hear.

These men are learning to be teachers of blind people. They are blindfolded and cannot see what they are eating. Which senses tell them what they are having for dinner?

Sometimes your mother tastes milk to see if it is sweet. When you are cracking and eating nuts, you may find spoiled ones. You cannot always tell that a nut is spoiled by looking at it. But your tasters tell you in time so that you do not swallow it. In this way your tasters sometimes keep you from harm. When you taste food and find that it has spoiled, you do not swallow it. If food that has spoiled gets into your stomach, it may make you sick.

Your senses tell you in many ways what is going on around you. You can see and hear. You can smell and taste your food. And you can feel things that you touch.

1. *Tell how your senses have helped you during the last hour.*
2. *Which senses tell you what is going on at a distance from your body?*
3. *What do your eyes tell you about a thing?*
4. *What happens in your eyes when you go from the bright sunlight into a dark room?*
5. *Smell and taste often work together to tell you what you are eating. How could you experiment with an onion to see if this is true?*
6. *Which senses help you tell if food is spoiled?*

What keeps the parts of your body working together?

EVERY PART of your body must keep working. Your heart must keep pumping your blood. Your muscles must keep moving your body. Your lungs must do their work. Suppose your lungs took an hour's rest, or your heart stopped work at five o'clock in the afternoon! All the other parts would stop working, too, and you could not live.

The director of your body is your brain, inside your skull. The other parts of your body do what the brain tells them to do.

Your senses are somewhat like telephones. They get messages from the world around you. But you do not really understand the messages until they are carried to your brain. Your *nerves* are the message carriers. They are like the wires in a telephone system. They run to and from every part of your body. Thousands of them go to your skin and other parts of your body. They carry messages to your brain. Then they carry messages back from the brain to your arms and legs and other parts of your body.

The nerves that connect your brain and the other parts of your body make up a large bundle called the spinal cord. The spinal cord, you remember, is in the hollow tube running through your backbone.

Suppose you are watching a circus parade. How do you think your nerves work? Let us see how your nerves act when you are watching the parade.

Listen! Do you hear the drums in the band? The parade is coming. The sound from the beating drums travels to your ears. Away goes the message along the nerves from your ears to your brain. You hear the people talking and the sound of the peanut wagon's whistle.

And that is not all. Your eyes are seeing things, too. Look at the red and white flags. Now the band is coming, and the horns are shining in the sun. Are those elephants that are following the band? Are those clowns in the yellow coats? Hundreds of messages have been carried from your eyes to your brain in these few minutes.

Everything that you see and hear makes you want to be nearer the parade so that you can see better. Your eyes see a fence. Your brain tells you that you could see better from the top of the fence. Your brain sends a message to your legs, and you run toward the fence. While you are running, you fall and bump your head. Nerves carry a message of pain to your brain. Your brain sends a message to your hand, and you rub the hurt spot.

There are still other nerves at work. You smell popcorn, see the popcorn

wagon, and buy a bag. As you eat the popcorn, nerves carry a message. And you can taste the popcorn. You say this must have been a very busy day for your brain and nerves. Every day is a busy day for them.

Perhaps you are wondering why the messages do not get mixed up when there are so many of them every minute. That is because messages can travel along nerves in only one direction. Some nerves carry messages from different parts of your body to your brain. Other nerves carry messages from your brain to different parts of your body. When your brain receives a message, it decides what to do. Then it sends a message along the nerves that carry messages from your brain to the different parts of your body telling them what to do. Your brain is the part of your body that does your thinking for you. It keeps the parts of your body working together. A brain is the best director that ever told anyone what to do. It can do many things at once and not get mixed up.

---

1. *What part of your body is the director?*
2. *Where is the director in your body?*
3. *Why does your body need a director?*
4. *How are messages carried to and from the brain?*

QUESTIONS TO ANSWER
---

1. How are each of these parts important to your body?

Joints   Muscles   Brain   Skin
Heart   Lungs   Teeth   Nerves

2. What must happen to food before your body can use it?

3. Describe how the blood carries two very important things around your body.

4. Which of the ways to discover things did you use in this unit?

5. What parts of your body have joints like the hinges on a door?

6. Why do you think that you are more intelligent than a dog?

7. What part of your body is like the central station of a telephone system? Tell why you think so.

8. What do we mean when we say that a food is hard to digest?

9. Why does your mother often tell you to eat your food slowly?

10. How is the food you eat like the gasoline that is used by an automobile engine?

11. Try to remember what happened this morning as you walked to school. Tell how the message carriers of your body worked so that you knew what was happening as you walked along.

1. Get a large joint from a meat market. Study the bone to find out
   a) What the inside looks like.
   b) How muscles are fastened to it.
   c) How it is fastened to another bone.
   d) How the blood gets inside the bone.

2. Make a list of five things you have done today. What parts of your body did you use in doing them?

3. Write a story telling how some of the bread you eat is changed and how it travels through your body until it gets into your big toe.

4. Make a list of the new science words you have learned in this unit and tell what each word means.

5. Look closely at the back of your hand to see how the blood vessels branch out.

6. Have your teacher show you where your pulse is and how to use the pulse to count how fast your heart is beating. Take your pulse when you are sitting down. Then jump up and down a few times and count your heartbeats again. What happens? Can you see how this helps your body?

7. Count how many breaths you take in a minute when you are sitting down. Now jump up and down a few times and count the number of breaths. What happens? How do you think this helps your body?

★ *In Unit Four You Will Learn* ★

★ *How the earth gets its light* ★ *What the shape of the earth is* ★
★ *How the earth moves* ★ *Why we have daylight and darkness* ★
★ *Why the earth is like a clock* ★ *What makes a year* ★ *How
the hours of daylight and darkness change during the year* ★
★ *Why summer days are warmer than winter days* ★

Why Do We Have Days and Nights?

WOULD YOU BELIEVE that day comes because a sun god rolls the sun into the sky? Would you believe that night comes because the god carries the sun away? Would you believe what a small boy once said about what makes night? "I know what makes night," he said. "The sun goes into my neighbor's woods. That makes night."

Of course, you know that night and day are not caused by a sun god. And you know that the sun does not go into a woods at night. But do you know what really does cause day and night?

Thousands of years ago people began to wonder why darkness came at night and why light came again every morning. They watched the sun as it seemed to move across the sky. They studied the earth, too. But it took them hundreds of years of study and careful watching to find out what causes day and night.

In this unit you will read about some of the very important things that people have learned about the earth and the sun. These things will help you understand why some of the time we have daylight and some of the time darkness on the earth.

How does the earth get its light?

HOW MANY WAYS can you think of to light a room? You can use electric lights. You can use lamps that burn gas or lamps that burn oil. You may even light the room with candles.

All of these lights are alike in one way. They are all very hot. The electric-light bulb is hot. So you can be sure that the thin, glowing wires inside must be hot, too. The wires in the electric-light bulb get so hot that

91

These jet-propelled planes are all the same size, but the ones that are far off look much smaller than the ones that are near.

they glow and light the room. The burning oil in the wick of the lamp gets so hot that it gives off light. Many kinds of materials give off light if they get hot enough. Have you ever seen a piece of iron that had become so hot that it glowed with a red or white light?

Now if someone asked you this question, what would you answer? "Why does the sun give light?" A good answer would be, "The sun gives light because it is very, very hot."

The sun that warms us and gives us light looks like a big yellow ball. It is made of very hot gases. Nothing on earth is so hot as the sun. The temperature of the outside of this glowing ball is about 100 times as hot as the temperature is on the hottest day on earth. The inside of the ball is thousands of times as hot as any fire you could ever make!

This ball of glowing, hot gases may not seem very large to you. You would probably guess that it is

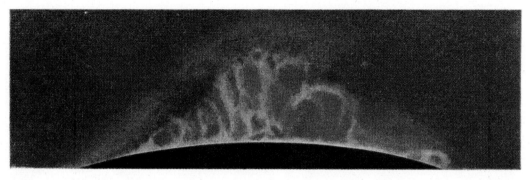

Scientists can take pictures of the sun that show some of the hot gases shooting far out from the edge.

much smaller than the earth we live on. But the sun is really not small. It is more than a million times as large as the earth! It looks small because it is so far away. Looking at the sun is like watching an airplane in the sky. When the airplane is far up in the sky, it looks very small. As it comes closer, it looks larger. A house or a ship or a tree or an automobile looks small when it is far away. The sun looks small because it is millions of miles away from us. It is 93 million miles from the earth to the sun.

You can understand how large the sun is if you make two drawings on the blackboard. Draw a circle a quarter of an inch across on the board. Next to it make another circle twenty-seven inches across. Write "The

Earth" over the small circle and "The Sun" over the large circle. This will help you see how big the sun is.

It is a good thing that our earth does not move any nearer the sun. If it did, we would all be baked by the heat. But do not worry. The sun and the earth will not get any closer together than they are. The sun will go on lighting and warming the earth for a long, long time.

But you know that the sun lights the part of the earth where we live only part of the time. Part of the time the place where we live is in darkness. Before you can understand why this is true, you need to know some things about the earth. You need to know the shape of the earth and how the earth moves.

1. *How do we know that the sun is very hot?*
2. *The sun is much larger than the earth. Why does it look so small?*
3. *Why is the sun important to us?*

What is the shape of the earth?

YOU HAVE PROBABLY heard that the earth is shaped like a big ball. You may have a hard time believing that we are walking around on a ball. But that is just what we are doing, for the earth really is shaped like a big ball.

Perhaps you are wondering why the earth does not seem round as you look out across the fields or the ocean. The earth does not look round because it is so very large. You can look miles away, and you cannot tell that the earth curves at all. You cannot see enough of the earth to be able to tell that it curves.

It is not surprising that hundreds of years ago most people thought the earth was flat like a table. They did not know as much about the earth as you will know when you have studied this book. They were sure that if they went far enough, they would come to the end of the earth. They were afraid to travel very far out on the ocean. They thought that the ship would come to the edge of the earth and fall off!

As people learned more and more about the earth, they began to wonder if it really were flat. Then a few thoughtful men began to believe that the earth was a big ball. Most people just laughed. They would not believe anything unless they could see it. And, of course, the earth looked flat to them just as it does to us.

But the men who thought the earth was a ball found a way to prove that they were right. They could not get far enough above the earth to see its shape. What do you think helped them find out the real shape of the earth?

In the days of long ago people did not do much traveling. Whenever a ship came back from sea, great crowds gathered at the shore to watch it. Some of the men who often went to watch the ships come in noticed something that seemed strange to them. They noticed that when the ship was far out, they could see only the top sails. As the ship came nearer, they could see the lower sails. As the ship came still closer, they could see the body of the ship.

This made them feel sure that the earth must be shaped like a ball. For if the earth were flat, all of the ship could be seen in the distance at the same time. It would just look bigger as it came nearer. Study the picture on page 94. Do you think these men were right?

If you do this experiment, you can understand how watching ships come in helped men learn that the earth is a big ball. Have someone hold a tiny boat on a globe, as you see in the picture. The boat should be on the opposite side of the globe from you so that you cannot see it. Then have the boat moved slowly around the globe toward you. Which part of the boat do you see first? Do the experiment again and watch closely. Name the different parts of the boat as you see them.

Now take the boat from the globe and put it at one end of a long table. Think of this table as a flat earth. Go to the other end of the table and stoop down until your eyes are on a level

with the table top. Watch the boat as someone moves it toward you. Do you see first just the top of it? Or do you see all parts of it at the same time? This experiment shows you that if the earth were flat, you would see all parts of a ship at the same time. Because the earth is a ball, you can see at first only the top parts of a ship as it comes toward you. Later you see the rest of it.

Christopher Columbus was one of the first sailors who believed that the earth was a ball. He believed that he could sail around it, and he tried to do so. But he landed on one of the islands off the southeastern coast of America.

Since the time of Columbus thousands of people have traveled around the earth. Aviators have flown around it in a few days. People have also gone very high above the earth in airplanes and balloons. They have been able to take pictures which show that the earth curves.

---

1. *Why do you think it took people so many years to find out that the earth is shaped like a ball?*
2. *How does the experiment show you that the earth is shaped like a ball?*
3. *What are two other reasons for believing that the earth is shaped like a ball?*

How does the earth move?

YOU HAVE LEARNED now that the earth is shaped like a ball. You also know that the sun gives it light. The sun shines all the time. But you know that the earth is dark part of the time at the place where you live. You must learn some other things about the earth before you can understand what causes day and night.

For a long time people wondered why we have days and nights. They knew that either the sun or the earth moved. Because they could see the sun in different places in the sky, they believed that the sun moved. They believed this for thousands of years. But some people began to wonder. They not only looked carefully at things, but they thought about the things they saw. They wondered if it was not the earth that moved instead of the sun.

At last, one of the people who had watched carefully proved that the earth spins around like a top. You can understand how the earth turns if you watch a top that is spinning. Turn a globe around fast and watch it spin, too. The top, the globe, and the earth all turn around on an *axis*.

You can understand what turning on an axis means if you try this experiment with an orange. Roll the orange on the table. Do you see that it turns this way and that way? Now push a short, stiff piece of wire through the orange and whirl the orange around on the wire. This time the orange does not turn in different directions. It keeps spinning around in the same place. It spins around on the piece of wire. That is what we mean when we say that something is turning on an axis.

Now take a quarter or some other coin and hold it on edge. Snap it with your finger so that it will spin on the table. Do you see that it turns just as the orange did except that there is no wire through the coin? The coin is spinning on its axis, too. Can you imagine that there is a line running through the coin like the wire that runs through the orange? The axis of the coin is an imaginary line on which the coin spins.

We say that the earth turns, or *rotates*, on an axis, too. It rotates from the west toward the east. It keeps rotating in the same direction just as the coin did. There is no rod running through the earth. The earth's axis is an imaginary line through the earth.

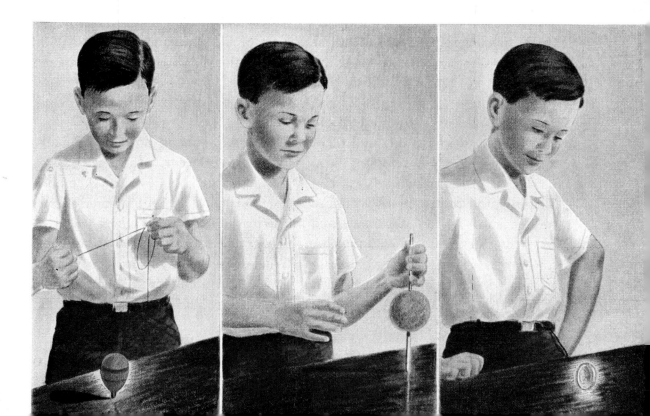

The ends of this imaginary line are called *poles*. One end is called the North Pole of the earth, and the other end is called the South Pole. Of course, there are no poles sticking out of the earth. Wherever you are on the earth, the direction north is always toward the North Pole. The direction south is always toward the South Pole.

---

1. *What does rotating on an axis mean?*
2. *How can an orange be made to spin on an axis?*
3. *Why is the spinning of the earth more like the spinning of a coin than the spinning of an orange?*
4. *What are the poles of the earth?*

Why do we have daylight and darkness?

Now you have learned three very important things to help you understand why we have darkness and daylight.

1. The sun lights the earth.
2. The earth is shaped like a ball.
3. The earth rotates on its axis.

A top spins around in a flash. The earth spins very fast, too. But the earth is so big that it takes twenty-four hours to spin around on its axis just once.

Now if you do this experiment, you can see why we have day and night once every twenty-four hours. You need a globe to use for the earth and a flashlight or some other light to use for the sun. Darken the room and hold the flashlight near the globe. Look at the globe. You see that only part of it is lighted. How much of it is lighted?

Remember that the flashlight is the sun and that the globe is the earth. Make a large chalk mark on the globe to show where you live on the earth. Turn the globe from west to east all the way around once on its axis. Do this slowly. What happens to the place where you live? Is it light part of the time and then dark part of the time? When the chalk mark is lighted, you are having daytime. When it is dark, you are having night-time.

This experiment shows that during one turn of the earth, the place where you live is light part of the time and then it is dark part of the time. When the place on the earth where you live faces the sun, you have daytime. When it faces away from the sun, you have night-time. You remember that the earth rotates once in twenty-four

hours. So during every twenty-four hours we have daytime once and night-time once.

Turn the globe so that the place where you live is having night. Now turn the globe slowly from west to east to show where your home will be when you are getting up in the morning. Turn it farther until it shows noon at your home. Keep turning the globe to show where your home is when school is out in the afternoon. Now turn the globe to show that it is almost night.

In the experiment which did you move, the globe or the light? You turned the globe, but the light did not move. It is this way with the earth and sun. The sun does not travel across the sky. The earth is turning on its axis from west to east.

That is what makes the sun seem to move across the sky. We first see the sun in the east in the morning. By noon the earth has turned more, and we see the sun overhead. By evening the earth has turned still more, and we see the sun low in the west. At last, we cannot see the sun at all. And it soon becomes dark. It is night.

It took people many years of study to find out that the earth is spinning around like a top. For a long time it seemed to them that the sun must surely be moving across the sky. You can see why they thought this.

Sometimes it is even hard for you to tell whether you are moving past some object or whether the object is moving past you. Have you ever been on a train and said this to yourself? "Is my train moving? Or is the train on the next track moving?" If your train starts smoothly so that you cannot feel it move, the train on the next track seems to be moving.

---

1. *Which of these things do you need to know to explain why we have day and night?*
   a) *Sometimes clouds hide the sun.*
   b) *The earth rotates on its axis.*
   c) *The earth gets its light from the sun.*
   d) *The earth is round like a ball.*
   e) *Some nights are very dark.*
   f) *Only half the earth can be lighted at one time.*
2. *How many times does the earth turn all the way around on its axis in one week?*
3. *In your own words tell why we have day and night.*

How is the earth like a clock?

THE EARTH IS the largest clock you have ever seen, and it is always on time. Does this idea puzzle you? Probably you have thought that a clock is a piece of machinery that tells us what time it is. You are right. A clock is a machine that tells us the time of day or night. All day and all night the hands of the clock turn slowly around, pointing first to one number and then to the next. You say that it is one o'clock, or two o'clock, and so on.

But what do you mean when you say that it is one o'clock or two o'clock? Suppose your clocks at home are wrong. Then how do you find out what the right time is? Perhaps you listen to the radio to find the right time. Or maybe your father says, "My watch is right. I set it by the clock in the jewelry store this morning." But how do the radio station and the jeweler get the right time?

If you are playing outdoors and do not have a watch with you, is there any way you can tell about what time it is? Probably you would look at the sun. If the sun is almost overhead, you say, "It is just about noon. It must be time for lunch." If the sun is low in the west, you say, "It must be late in the afternoon. The sun is almost down."

That is the way people used to tell time long ago, before clocks were

made. They used the sun as a clock. You really tell time that way even when you look at a clock. When you look at the clock, the clock is really telling you where the sun is. Now let us see why that is true.

You know that it takes the earth twenty-four hours to turn all the way around on its axis. When the earth has gone halfway around, we say that twelve hours have passed. When it turns the rest of the way around, another twelve hours have passed.

When the earth has made one complete turn around on its axis, we say that a day has passed. We divide the day into twenty-four equal parts, called hours. A day is made up of the hours of daylight and darkness. But how can we tell when the earth has

made one complete turn? We cannot see it turn.

If you shut your eyes on a merry-go-round, you cannot tell how far you have turned or how many times you have turned around. But if a friend of yours is standing beside the merry-go-round, you can look at him and count the times you pass him. Then you know how many times you have gone around. You can also tell when you have gone halfway around.

We watch the sun to tell when the earth has turned once. We can also tell how far the earth has turned at any time. We can also watch the stars to find out how far the earth has turned.

In the city of Washington there are several very important clocks. They

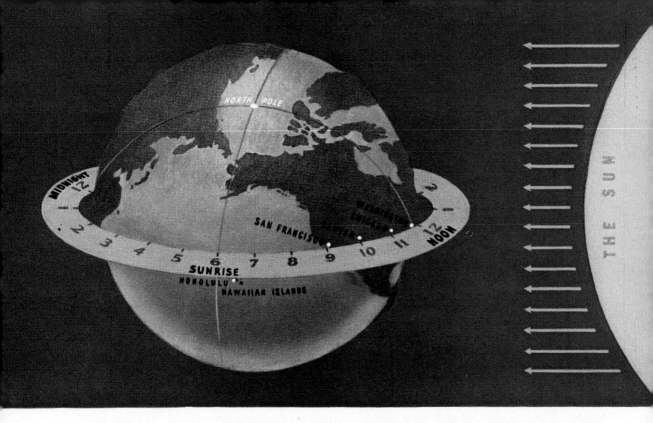

When the earth has turned so that it is noon in Washington, what time is it in Chicago? What time is it where you live?

are always being checked to see if they show the correct time. Every clear night a scientist looks at the stars through a *telescope* and finds out what time it is. Then he looks to see if these clocks show the correct time.

Several times a day he sends signals by radio and telegraph to all parts of the country to let people know what the correct time is. Radio stations and jewelers can get the right time, and people can set their clocks. Twelve o'clock noon is one of the times when the signals are sent out.

When it is twelve o'clock in the city of Washington, is it twelve o'clock

everywhere in the United States? You can answer this question by doing an experiment. Use a flashlight and globe as you did in the experiment on page 98. Turn the globe so that it is noon in Washington. That is the time the sun is highest in the sky.

Now if you look at Chicago, Denver, and San Francisco on the globe, you can see that it will not be noon in these cities. Before it will be noon in Chicago, you must turn the globe some more. When it is twelve o'clock in Washington, it is eleven o'clock in Chicago, ten o'clock in Denver, and nine o'clock in San Francisco. This means that you must turn your watch

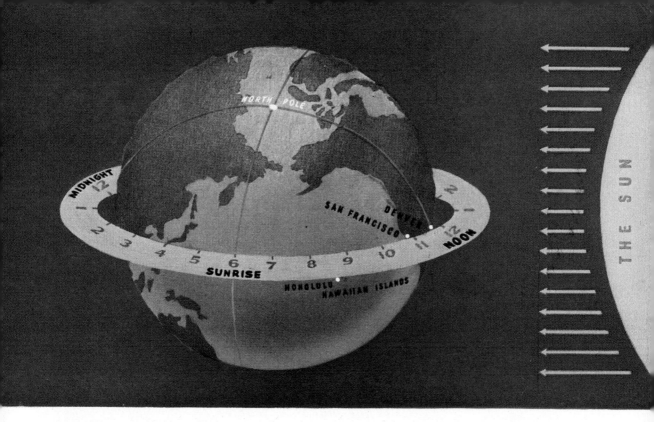

Now the earth has turned so that it is noon in Denver. What time is it in San Francisco? What time is it in Honolulu?

back when you cross the country from east to west. When you travel from west to east, you must turn your watch ahead.

When you look at your clock and see that it is twelve o'clock noon, you are really finding the time when the sun is highest in the sky. At three o'clock in the afternoon you know that it is three hours past the time when

the sun was highest in the sky. You know that it will take twenty-four hours for the earth to turn before the sun is at the same point again.

Do you see how the earth is used as our clock? Your clock at home may run too fast or too slow. But the earth keeps on rotating at the same speed year after year. It rotates once every twenty-four hours.

1. Explain how the earth is like a clock. If you have a globe, use it to show what you mean.
2. Why is the time different in different parts of the country?
3. How many times has the earth turned around on its axis since yesterday at this time? How many hours have passed?

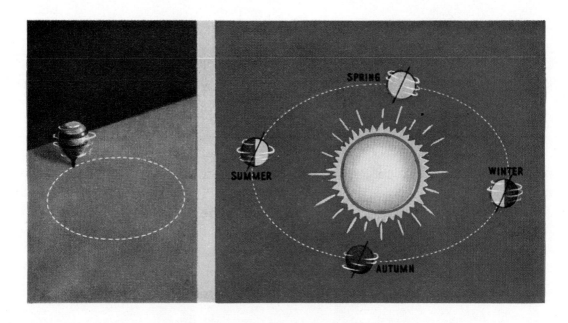

What makes a year?

YOU HAVE LEARNED what makes a day. It is the time the earth takes to turn all the way around once on its axis. But you do not measure your age in days. You measure it in years. And years are measured by another way in which the earth moves.

Look at the picture on this page. It shows you that the earth is doing something else besides spinning like a top. It is traveling around the sun all the time, just as you move around the center of a merry-go-round. Sometimes when you spin a top, it moves slowly around almost in a circle. Can you see that the top and the earth are both making two kinds of movements? Each one is spinning on its axis and traveling in a circle, too.

You know that it takes twenty-four hours for the earth to turn around once on its axis. But it takes 365¼ days for the earth to travel all the way around the sun. A year is the time it takes the earth to travel, or *revolve*, once around the sun. This means that if you are ten years old, the earth has revolved around the sun ten times since you were born. If anyone asked you how you measure your age, your answer could be "I get a year older every time the earth revolves all the way around the sun."

Look again at the picture on this page. Do you see the names of the four seasons of the year? Suppose that the earth begins its trip around the sun in January. When summer comes, has the earth traveled halfway around the sun, three quarters of the way, or one quarter of the way? How far has it traveled when spring comes?

Do you see that in summer the earth is on the opposite side of the sun from where it was in winter? When is it on the opposite side from where it was in autumn? The seasons tell us how far the earth has traveled around the sun since the year began. Each year is divided into four seasons. When four seasons have passed, the earth has revolved once around the sun.

---

1. *What two movements does the earth make?*
2. *Which movement gives us days? Which gives us years?*
3. *How many times has the earth traveled around the sun since you were born? Since you started going to school?*
4. *How many times does the earth rotate on its axis while it revolves once around the sun?*

How do the hours of daylight and darkness change during the year?

HAVE YOU EVER read this little poem?

In winter, I get up at night
And dress by yellow candlelight.
In summer, quite the other way,
I have to go to bed by day.

What does the poem tell you about daylight and darkness during the year? Of course, you have noticed that as the year passes by, some days have many more daylight hours than others. Summer days have more hours of daylight than winter days. In summer, the sun is up long before you get out of bed. And after supper the sun still gives light enough for you to play outdoors. At seven o'clock on summer evenings you can see well enough to play a game of ball.

Winter days have fewer hours of daylight than summer days. In winter, the sun does not come up until you are having breakfast. And the sun goes down before you eat your supper. You do not play outdoors after supper. You stay indoors and read or play games. If you go outdoors, it is dark.

You can find out just how much the amount of daylight changes by keeping a record of the hours of daylight and darkness. Daylight begins when

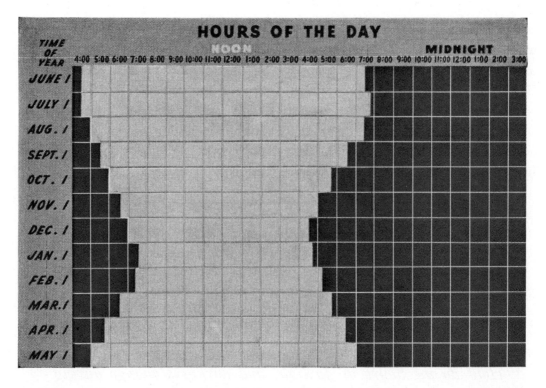

HOURS OF THE DAY

we first see the sun in the east. And it ends when we no longer see the sun in the west. It may be hard for you to tell the exact time of the sunrise every morning. You probably do not get up early enough. And clouds or buildings often hide the sun. But the time of sunrise and sunset for each day is printed in the newspapers.

Here is a record that some children once made of the number of daylight hours. You can see that there are twenty-four squares in each row across the chart. Each square is an hour of time. The yellow squares show the number of daylight hours. The blue squares show the number of hours of darkness. The date beside each row of squares shows the time of the year. Look carefully at the chart and then answer these questions.

---

1. *Which four months have the most daylight?*
2. *Which four months have the least daylight?*
3. *Is there much daylight or little daylight on your birthday?*
4. *In which months are the hours of daylight and darkness about the same?*

Why are summer days warmer than winter days?

SUMMER DAYS have more hours of daylight than winter days. They are different in another way, too. Summer days are much warmer than winter days. Can you think of one reason why this is true? You know that the sun gives us light and heat. The longer the sun shines on our part of the earth, the longer we get heat from the sun. So, in summer, we get more heat from the sun.

In winter, there are fewer hours of daylight. So the hours of darkness are longer. The sun does not shine on our part of the earth for so many hours. So the earth gets less light and heat from the sun, and the days and nights are cold.

There is another reason why the days are warmer in summer and colder in winter. It is because of the way the sun shines on the earth. The girl in the picture on this page is doing an experiment that will help you see why this is true. You can do the experiment, too, if you have a flashlight and a cardboard tube or some heavy paper.

Turn the flashlight on and put it inside the tube. Have the room as dark as possible. Hold the flashlight straight up and down above the table. Then slant it as the girl in the picture on the right is doing. Which spot is brighter, the larger one or the smaller one?

When the flashlight is slanted, the light is spread over a larger space than when it is held straight up and down. So the spot is brighter when the flashlight is straight up and down above the table.

Perhaps you have noticed that the sun is higher in the sky and straighter overhead during summer days than during winter days. There is an easy way to show that the sun is higher in the sky in summer than it is in winter. You know that when the light strikes you, your body makes a shadow. If it shines on you from nearly overhead, you make a short shadow. If it shines on you from lower down in the sky, your shadow is longer. So if you want to tell when the sun is highest, you can measure the length of your shadow at the same time of day in summer and in winter. Then you can tell when the sun is highest in the sky.

If you have ever watched your shadow as you walked under a street light at night, you understand how the length of a shadow changes. When the light is almost straight over your head, your shadow is short. If you walk away so that the light is not over your head, your shadow gets longer.

You do not need to be outdoors to see how shadows change. You can make them change right in your schoolroom by using a light for the sun and a yardstick to make the shadow. Set the yardstick up on one end. Then hold the light nearly above the yardstick. Is the shadow long or

short? Now move the light to one side of the yardstick. Does the shadow get longer?

In the picture on page 108, the children are swimming in a pond late on a summer afternoon. The children and the tree make short shadows. In the picture on this page, the children are skating on the pond at about the same time on a winter afternoon. See what long shadows the tree and the children make now. What does this tell you about the sun in winter? The sun is lower in the sky and not so straight overhead in winter.

The sun is straightest overhead in summer. So the earth gets more heat in summer. The earth gets the most heat when the sun is straightest overhead and when it shines the longest. So the days are warmer in summer than they are during the other seasons.

1. *Give two reasons why summer days are warmer than winter days.*
2. *How does your shadow tell you when the sun is straightest overhead?*
3. *During which season of the year will shadows be the shortest? During which season will they be longest?*

This girl is looking at a sundial. Find out how sundials are used for telling time.

QUESTIONS TO ANSWER

1. Why have people changed their minds about what makes day and night?

2. Which of these things did people need to know before they could understand why summer is warmer than winter? Explain your answer.

a) The earth goes around the sun.

b) The days are longer in summer than in winter.

c) The sun is straighter overhead in summer than in winter.

d) The earth turns on its axis.

e) The sun is far from the earth.

f) The earth gets the most heat when the sun is straightest overhead.

3. How does the change in the hours of daylight and darkness make a difference to baseball players, farmers, drivers of milk wagons, and boys carrying newspapers?

4. Think of as many things as you can that would happen on the earth if the sun did not shine at all.

5. How do you know that the earth turns on its axis from west to east?

6. About how many times has the earth turned around on its axis since you were born?

7. Why is it important for the men who run railroad trains to know exactly what time it is?

1. Ask a jeweler how he finds out the correct time. How often does he get the correct time?

2. Lay a sheet of paper where the sun will shine on it all day. Have the long way of the paper pointing north and south. Stick a pin straight up and down in the paper at the south edge. Draw a line right on the shadow. Keep on drawing lines along the shadow every hour. How does the length of the shadow change? Can you tell about what time of day it is in this way?

3. Measure your shadow in the morning, then at noon, and again in the late afternoon. Explain what you find out.

4. Find out how people told time before they had clocks. Find out whether people still use any of these ways of telling time.

5. What day of the year has the most daylight? What day of the year has the least daylight?

6. Find out what two days of the year have exactly the same amount of daylight and darkness.

★ *Unit Five Will Tell You* ★

★ *What a star is* ★ *What a constellation is* ★ *Why the constellations seem to move* ★ *How the moon is different from the stars* ★ *What the moon is like* ★ *Why the moon seems to change its shape* ★ *What a planet is* ★ *What a shooting star is* ★

What Can We See in the Sky at Night?

HAVE YOU EVER seen a sun at night? Of course you have. You have seen hundreds of suns. You have seen so many suns at night that it would take you a long time to count them. Does this seem strange to you?

In the daytime you see only one sun. It is the great hot ball of glowing gases that gives us heat and light. But at night, if you look up into the sky, you can see hundreds of shining, twinkling suns.

What is a star?

YOU HAVE ALWAYS called these twinkling suns *stars*, and they are stars. But they are suns, too. Suns and stars are the same. Each star is a big ball of glowing gases. These gases are very, very hot, just like the gases in our sun. They give light, just as the hot gases in our sun do. It is this light that you see up in the sky at night.

Perhaps you wonder why these stars do not look like our sun. It is because they are so far away. They are hundreds and thousands of times as far away from the earth as our sun is. You know that automobile lights look like tiny dots when they are a long way down the street. As they come closer, they look larger and larger.

If these far-off stars should come as close as our sun, they would look larger, too. Many of them are much larger than our sun. Some of them would almost cover the whole sky

113

This bar of steel has been heated until it gives off a yellow light.

if they were as close to us as our sun is! If our sun were as far away as any of the other stars, it would look like a tiny point of light.

If you have ever looked closely at the stars, you may have noticed that they are not all the same color. Some are reddish, some are yellowish, and some are bluish-white. If you try this experiment, you can explain why the stars have different colors.

Find an old steel knitting needle or a piece of iron wire about a foot long. With a pair of pliers hold the steel or iron in a very hot flame. Keep it in the flame and watch the color of the steel or iron change.

Before you put the metal into the flame, it is cold. It does not give off any light or heat. Soon after you put it into the fire, it begins to get red-hot. It gives off a red light. As you keep heating the metal, it gets hotter and hotter until it is yellow. Then it gives off a yellow light. When the metal is yellow, it is hotter than it was when it gave off the red light.

If you could heat the steel or iron still hotter, it would get so hot that it would give off a bluish-white light. It would then be very, very hot. Perhaps you can see now why stars have different colors. Some stars are much hotter than others. Now when you look at the stars, you can tell the hot-test stars from the stars that are not quite so hot.

You know from your experiment with the metal that red stars are hot. But they are not so hot as some of the others. Have you found yellow stars in the sky at night? They are hotter than the red stars. There are other stars in the sky that give bluish-white light. You know that they are hotter than either the red stars or the yellow stars.

Perhaps tonight you may look up at the sky and see a star that is bluish-white. You may say to yourself, "That is a very, very hot star. It is hotter than the yellow stars and much hotter than the red ones."

1. *How is our sun like the other stars?*
2. *Is the star that we call our sun as hot as a bluish-white star? Is it as hot as a red star? How do you know?*
3. *Why does the sun give light?*
4. *Some of the stars are larger than our sun. Why do they look smaller than the sun?*
5. *List the colors of the stars, beginning with the hottest stars.*

What is a constellation?

SUPPOSE YOU GO outdoors tonight and look at the stars. Soon after the sun goes down, they begin to come out. At first, you see only a few stars. As it gets darker, you see more and more of them. At last, the whole sky seems to be filled with hundreds of shining points.

Look closely, and you may see that some of these stars look as though they are grouped together. One of these groups of stars has the shape of

a huge dipper. You can find it easily if you face toward the north and look up at the sky. You will see the bowl of the dipper and the long, curved handle. This group of stars is called the *Big Dipper*.

Look near this dipper in the northern sky, and you may see a group of stars that has the shape of a smaller dipper. You can see the two dippers in the picture at the top of the page.

Scientists call a group of stars a *constellation*. The constellations, or groups of stars, have names. The Big Dipper is part of one of these groups of stars. It is part of a large constellation called *Ursa Major*. Ursa Major means Big Bear.

The constellation that looks like a small dipper is usually called the *Little Dipper*. The Little Dipper is also called *Ursa Minor,* which means Little Bear.

You are probably wondering why a group of stars is called Ursa Major, or Big Bear. For hundreds of years people have watched the stars and studied the constellations. The shepherds of long ago discovered these star groups as they watched over their sheep on the hillsides. The sky was almost the only thing the shepherds had to look at through the long nights. They wondered what the stars were and how so many of them came to be up in the sky.

The shepherds made up stories about these constellations as they watched the starry sky night after night. They imagined that some of the groups of stars had the shapes of animals. They thought other groups made pictures of kings or queens or hunters. The Indians made up stories about these groups of stars, too. The stories about the constellations are very, very old. Today we know that they are not true, but people once believed them. We still use the names that the people of long ago gave to the groups of stars.

One of the most interesting stories is about the constellations of Ursa Major and Ursa Minor. It tells about a princess who once lived on the earth, and about Jupiter, the king of the gods, who lived in the sky. The queen of the gods became very angry with the princess. So she had the princess changed into a bear.

One day when the son of the princess was hunting, he came upon this bear in the woods. The prince did not know that the bear was his mother. He was just going to kill the bear when Jupiter stopped him. Then Jupiter changed the young man into a little bear, took him by the tail, and threw him into the sky. After that, Jupiter took the big bear and threw her up into the sky near her son.

Now you can understand how one constellation came to be called Ursa Major, or Big Bear, and why the other constellation came to be called Ursa Minor, or Little Bear. Ursa is an old,

old word for bear. Major means large, and minor means small. Look at the picture on this page. It shows how people thought they could see the shapes of two bears in the sky. Do you see that the handle of the Big Dipper makes the tail of the Big Bear? What part of the Little Dipper makes the tail of the Little Bear? You may have to turn the picture upside down to see the Little Dipper clearly.

There are seven bright stars in the group of stars called the Big Dipper. In the early evening in February and March you will find the Big Dipper standing on its handle in the northeastern sky. Four bright stars make the bowl of the Big Dipper, and three bright stars make its handle.

The constellations are in the positions shown in this picture about 8 o'clock in the evening during the month of March.

Look at the picture on this page and find the stars at the front of the bowl. They are numbered 1 and 2. These stars are very important ones to know. They will help you tell which direction is north, and they will also help you find other constellations in the sky. They are called the *pointers.* If you draw a line from 1 to 2 and then draw the line on across the sky, you will see that it points toward another bright star. This star is called the *North Star. Polaris* is another name for the North Star.

When you look toward this star, you are looking north. It is called the North Star because it is always in the north. Sometimes the North Star is called the *Pole Star* because it is almost straight above the earth's North Pole. Scientists usually call the Pole Star Polaris.

The constellation of the Little Dipper is easy to find if you have learned to find the North Star. The North Star is at the end of the handle of the Little Dipper. Study the picture and see how easy it is to find the Little Dipper after you have found the North Star. There are seven stars in the Little Dipper, just as there are in the Big Dipper. But they are not nearly so bright as the stars in the Big Dipper.

Find the Big Dipper in the picture on page 116. Find the North Star and the Little Dipper. On a clear night you can find them in the sky just as you have found them in the picture.

After you have learned to find the Big Dipper and the Little Dipper, you will want to find other groups of stars. Another constellation that is easy to

find is the group of stars that looks like a W. The W is made of five bright stars. This constellation is called *Cassiopeia*, the name of a queen of long ago. Sometimes it is called Cassiopeia's Chair. In the picture you will see that the letter W makes a chair for the queen.

So far, we have looked only at the stars toward the north. Now let us turn around and see what we can find in the southern part of the sky. Here we find a constellation that has some of the brightest stars in the sky. It is called *Orion*.

Long ago, people thought that this group of stars had the shape of a mighty hunter. They named it Orion after a famous hunter in their stories. They imagined that the hunter in the sky had a belt with a shining sword hanging from it. In his right hand they thought he held up a big club.

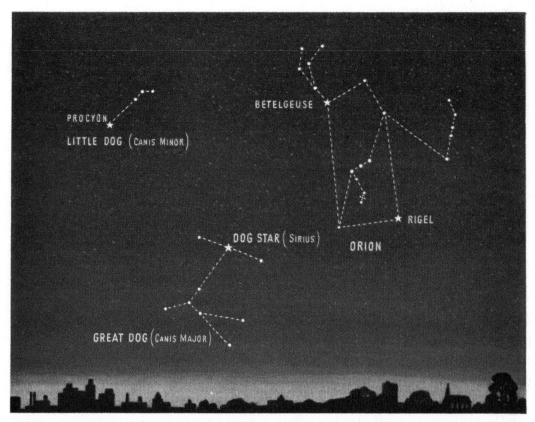

During the winter months face south, and you can easily see Orion. Perhaps you can find the dogs, too.

On his left arm he held a lion's skin for a shield. Behind the hunter were his two dogs. In the picture on this page you will find the two constellations that make the dogs. What are the names of these constellations? What is the name of the brightest star in each constellation?

Orion is a large constellation. It has more bright stars than any other constellation. To find Orion, look in wintertime toward the south until you see three bright stars in a row.

These stars are Orion's belt. Find them in the picture. Just below them are a few small stars close together. They show where the sword hangs from the hunter's belt. Below the belt and a little to the right is a large, bright star. This star is called *Rigel*. It shows the lifted knee of Orion. There are only six stars in the sky that are brighter than Rigel.

Now look above the belt and a little to the left, and you will see another large, bright star. This one is called *Betelgeuse*. It marks Orion's shoulder. Betelgeuse is a very big star. It is many, many times as large as our sun. It is a good thing for us that Betelgeuse is very far away from the earth, because it would very quickly burn us up if it were as close to us as the sun is.

You can be sure that you have found Betelgeuse and Rigel if you will notice their colors. Rigel is bluish-white, while Betelgeuse is reddish in color. Can you tell which of these stars is hotter?

If you are out looking at the constellations on a very clear night, you will probably see something that looks like a bright pathway of light going from north to south across the sky. This is the *Milky Way*. It is called the Milky Way because it looks as if someone had spilled a pail of milk across the sky. But scientists know that the Milky Way looks so

bright because it is made up of many, many millions of stars that are giving off light. Look at the picture at the beginning of this unit. Can you find the Milky Way?

---

1. *Name four constellations and tell how you would help someone find them.*
2. *Draw the Big Dipper and show how to find the North Star by using the pointers.*
3. *Draw the constellation Orion on the blackboard and tell the names of the brightest stars in it.*
4. *Which constellations that you have learned about are in the southern sky? Which are in the northern sky?*
5. *Write three things you have learned about each of these.*
   Constellations   The North Star   Orion

Why do the constellations seem to move?

ON SOME CLEAR NIGHT, as soon as the stars are out, notice just where Orion is in the sky. Then just before you go to bed look at this constellation again. Was Orion farther toward the west the second time you saw it? If you stayed up much later to see Orion, you would not find it. It would be out of sight!

The same thing happens when you are watching the sun. You know that we first see the sun in the east, and at the end of the day we see it disappear in the west. But the sun does not move around the earth, nor do the stars. We see the star groups in different places at different times because the earth turns on its axis.

You can see why this is true if you will do this experiment. On the underside of a dark blue or black umbrella paint the Big Dipper, Little Dipper, and Cassiopeia. Use the picture at the top of this page to show where to put these constellations. Put the North Star against the rod that goes through the center of the umbrella.

Have one of your classmates hold the handle of the umbrella on the globe at the North Pole. Be sure that the globe will turn but the umbrella will not. Then cut out a little cardboard boy and paste it on the globe so that it is standing near the place where you live.

The Big Dipper can be used as a clock because it seems to move around Polaris. But the Dipper moves in the opposite direction from the hour hands on a clock. The stars are in the positions shown in the picture about the first week in March.

Now stand beside the globe where the cardboard boy is pasted and look up at the umbrella sky. Is the Big Dipper at the right or at the left of the North Star? Turn the globe slowly about halfway around and follow the cardboard boy. Is the Big Dipper now at the right or at the left of the North Star?

The experiment shows that when the globe is turned, the stars are seen in different parts of the sky. If the globe did not turn, the stars would be found in the same part of the sky.

1. Does the experiment show that the constellations change their positions because they are moving or because the earth is moving?
2. What does the picture on this page show?
3. How can you tell from the picture that the Dipper moves in the opposite direction from the hour hands on a clock?

This railroad-crossing sign is made of pieces of metal that reflect the light from automobile headlights. The metal markers at the left side of the road reflect light, too. Smooth, light-colored materials reflect more light than dark, rough ones.

How is the moon different from the stars?

WHILE YOU HAVE been watching the stars, you must have noticed something else in the sky. It shines brighter than anything else in the sky except our sun. Of course, it is the *moon*. The moon is nearer to us than any of the stars. It is only about 240,000 miles from us, while the sun is 93 million miles away.

The moon is round like a ball. But it is not hot like the sun and the stars. So it cannot give off its own light. Do you know how we can see it even if it does not give off its own light?

Have you ever driven along a country road at night and noticed the signs that shine when light from your automobile strikes them? These signs that read "Stop" or "Curve" are often made with little pieces of metal or glass. At night, the light from your car shines on the signs, and they glow as if they had electric-light bulbs on them.

If you hold a mirror so that the sunlight strikes it, you can make a bright spot of light on the wall. The mirror seems to be making its own light.

But the road signs and the mirror have no light of their own. We say that they *reflect* light. Reflect means throw back. The signs reflect the light from the automobile. The mirror reflects the light of the sun.

The moon reflects light in the same way. Light from the sun strikes the moon, and the moon reflects the light. We see the moon because the light from the sun is reflected from the moon to us.

---

1. What does reflect mean?
2. How is the moon different from a star?
3. Why is moonlight really sunlight?
4. Why do the pieces of metal in the road look brighter than the road?

What is the moon like?

DID YOU EVER SEE "the man in the moon"? Of course, we know that the face on the moon is really not a face at all. But do you know what it is? Let us see if we can find out.

If you went for a long hike on the moon, you would find it very rough walking in many places. There are long ranges of mountains with deep valleys. And there are big holes in the

If you watch the moon every few days for a month, you will see that it has these shapes. The thin slice that you see first is usually called the new moon. When it is round, it is called the full moon.

tops of some of the mountains. On some parts of the moon there are long, level plains.

On page 125 is a picture of the moon. You can see mountains, valleys, and plains. When light from the sun strikes the moon, these mountains make big, long shadows. We can see these shadows. We like to imagine that they make the face of a man. We call this man the "man in the moon."

Scientists have studied the moon with huge telescopes like the one on page 134. Telescopes make the moon look nearer and larger. Sometimes a scientist puts a camera on the telescope and takes pictures of the moon.

The picture of the moon on page 125 was taken this way. That is why you can see the mountains and valleys so plainly. Scientists have given names to many of the mountains, valleys, and plains. They have even made maps of the moon.

Even if you could get to the moon, you could not live there. Do you know why? If you remember what you learned in Unit Two, you will understand why. There is no air on the moon. So, of course, there would not be any oxygen for you to breathe. There is no water, either. With no air and no water, you could never live there. There are no living things on the moon.

1. *Why are there no living things on the moon?*
2. *Why do we see shadows on the moon?*
3. *Which of these things are on the moon?*
   Trees   Mountains   Lakes   Birds   Shadows

These pictures show how the moon looks after it has been full and round. The thin slice that we see last is called the old moon. For a few days before the next new moon, we cannot see the moon at all.

Why does the moon seem to change its shape?

As you watch the moon, you notice that it does not always seem to have the same shape. Sometimes it looks thin and curved, like the first picture on page 126. Then on the following nights it seems to grow larger and larger. In about two weeks it looks round. What happens then? Look at the pictures on this page and see what happens after it looks round.

You have often seen the moon when it has the different shapes shown in the pictures. Let us see if we can find out why the moon seems to have these different shapes each month.

You know that the moon does not give its own light. We see it because it reflects sunlight. You remember that the sun always lights half of the earth. The sun always lights half of the moon, too. But from where we are on the earth, we cannot always see all of the lighted part of the moon. Sometimes we cannot see any of the lighted part.

When we cannot see the moon at all, we are looking at the side that is not lighted. Scientists call this dark side of the moon the *new moon*. But we usually call the first part that we can see each month the new moon. This is just a thin slice of the lighted part.

When we see half of the lighted part, we say that the moon is half full. Or we call it a *half moon*. When we can see all of the lighted half, the moon looks round to us. We call it a *full moon*. At the end of the month we again see only a thin slice of the lighted part. This is called the *old moon*.

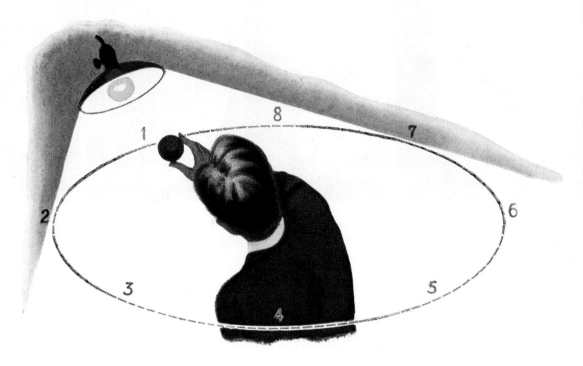

Perhaps you can understand this better if you do an experiment. Get a bright light. Place or have someone hold the light as shown in the picture. Imagine that this light is the sun. You are the earth. Hold a small ball like a tennis ball at arm's length from you.

The ball is the moon. Stand with your face toward the light and hold the ball between you and the light as the boy in the picture on this page is doing. Is all of the ball lighted? Can you see the part that is lighted?

Now turn slowly around and stop at each one of the numbered places. Can you always see all of the lighted part? Draw pictures of the lighted parts that you can see. Compare your pictures with the pictures on pages 126 and 127. Do they show the same shapes as the lighted parts in the photographs of the moon?

Try to find a calendar that has the different shapes of the moon on it. The new moon will be shown as a black ball or as a very small part of the moon. As the days of the month pass, we can see more and more of the moon. At last, the moon will be round and full. Then the lighted part will slowly get smaller and smaller again.

The shapes of the moon are put on the calendar to show you when the moon is full, when you can see only part of it, and when you cannot see it at all.

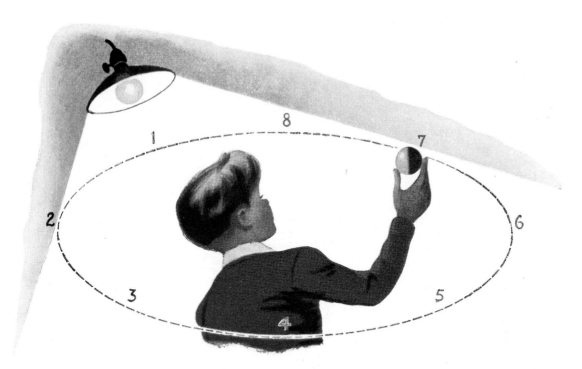

The Indians did not have calendars. They used the moon to tell how much time had passed. The moon goes through its changes in shape once in about twenty-eight days, or about four weeks. This is almost a month. As you know, there are twelve months in every year. The Indians used to call a month a "moon." To tell about a long journey that took many months, they might say, "We traveled for many moons."

1. What does the experiment show you about the moon?
2. Which sentences below describe the moon? Which sentence describes a star?
   a) It reflects light from the sun.
   b) It is a hot ball of gas.
   c) It seems to change its shape.
   d) It is closer to the earth than any of the stars.
   e) It has deep valleys and high mountains.
3. How long does it take from one new moon to the next one?
4. Look at a calendar that has the shapes of the moon on it. On what date is the moon full this month? On what date is it new next month?

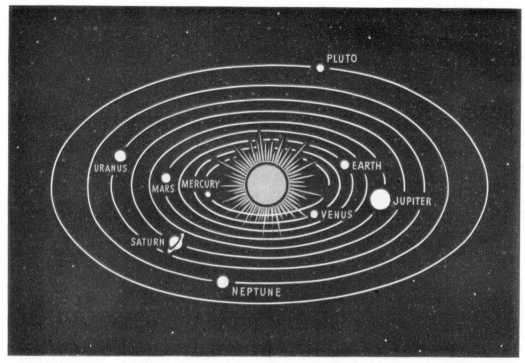

As the planets travel around the sun, each planet always stays in its own path.

What is a planet?

IF YOU LOOK UP into the sky at night, you may see other lights that are not stars. Like the moon, they do not give off light of their own. They reflect light from the sun just as the moon does. These other lights you may see in the sky at night are called *planets*. Planets look like stars, but they are really quite different. All planets travel around the sun, but no stars do. A planet does not give off light of its own as a star does.

There are millions of stars, but there are only nine *known* planets. We say *known* planets, because until a few years ago scientists thought there were only eight planets. Then they found another planet. Perhaps, as scientists watch the sky, they may find still more planets. Almost every day scientists discover something new about the world we live in.

How would you like to live on a planet? You may be surprised to learn that you do live on one. The earth is one of the nine planets. It does not give off its own light. And it travels around the sun, as you know. Two of the planets are closer to the sun than the earth is. Study the picture on page 130 and tell which planets they are. Six of the planets are farther from the sun than the earth is. Find the names of these six planets.

The planet nearest to the sun is called *Mercury*. You remember that it takes our planet, the earth, a year to travel around the sun. A year on the other planets is the time it takes these planets to travel around the sun, too. Some of the planets are nearer to the sun than the earth is. It does not take them so long to travel around the sun. Their year is shorter than ours. Some are farther away from the sun than the earth is. Their year is longer than ours. Mercury is so close to the sun that it has a much shorter journey around the sun. Its year is only eighty-eight days long. How many days are there in our year?

The planet next to Mercury in nearness to the sun is *Venus*. Venus takes 225 days to go around the sun. There are only two things in the sky that are brighter than Venus. Do you know what they are? One is the sun. The other is the moon. Venus is the third brightest. When you see it in the sky at night, you may think that it is the bright light of an airplane.

Venus is a beautiful planet. You can sometimes see it in the western sky just after sunset. Then it is called the "evening star."

You have probably heard people talk about the "evening star" or the "morning star." These "stars" are really planets that can be seen after sunset or before sunrise. Sometimes Venus is an "evening star." At other times, Venus is a "morning star." You would have to get up before sunrise to see it.

Venus is sometimes called the earth's twin, because it is almost the same size as the earth. Scientists cannot find out what Venus is really like, because there are so many clouds around it. But scientists do know that Venus seems to change its shape, just as the moon does. The picture on this page shows how Venus looks at different times.

The planet on the left is Jupiter. The picture on the right shows Saturn and its rings.

Farther out from the sun is *Mars*. It is farther from the sun than Mercury, Venus, and the earth are. Mars is much smaller than the earth. The earth would make six planets the size of Mars. But the year on Mars is almost twice as long as the earth's year, because Mars is farther away from the sun and takes more time to travel around it. Mars looks red.

Next beyond Mars comes *Jupiter,* the largest of all the planets. It is still farther away from the sun than Mercury, Venus, Earth, and Mars. Jupiter is larger than all of the other planets put together. It is about a thousand times as big as the earth. Jupiter is so far away from the sun that it takes almost twelve of our years to travel once around the sun. If you lived on Jupiter, you would have only one birthday every twelve years!

Next beyond Jupiter, and still farther away from the sun, is a planet called *Saturn.* Saturn is a very beautiful planet to see through a telescope. Study the picture of Saturn on this page. Do you see how it is different from any of the other planets? It has rings. Sometime, when you learn more about Saturn, you will find out many interesting things about these rings.

Because Saturn is still farther away from the sun than Jupiter is, it has even a longer year than Jupiter. It takes Saturn nearly thirty of our years to go around the sun once.

After Saturn we come to *Uranus* and then *Neptune*. It takes Uranus eighty-four years to go around the sun. The year on Neptune is almost 165 times as long as our year on earth. Farthest away from the sun of all is a planet that was discovered only a few years ago. Its name is *Pluto.* Pluto is so far away from the sun that it takes 250 of our years to travel around the sun once. Pluto cannot be seen without the help of a telescope. It is so hard to see this planet that scientists know very little about it.

---

1. *In what two ways are planets different from stars?*
2. *Name the planets. Begin with the one closest to the sun and end with the one farthest away.*
3. *Why do we say, "There are nine known planets"?*
4. *Tell the name of the planet that*
   a) *Is closest to the sun.*
   b) *Has rings.*
   c) *Is the brightest of the planets.*
   d) *Is called the earth's twin.*
   e) *Is farthest from the sun.*
   f) *Is the largest planet.*
   g) *Was discovered last.*

Are there living things on the planets?

HAVE YOU EVER wondered whether there are living things on any of the other planets? We are sure that there are living things on one of the planets. You know which one it is. It is the earth.

Even the wisest scientists do not know whether there are living things on the other planets. But they have found good reasons for believing that nothing could stay alive on most of them. Mercury is too close to the sun. It is so hot that a lead pipe would melt quickly on it. So scientists are sure that it would be too hot for anything to stay alive. Most of the other planets have no air on them. No one could live on these planets. Pluto and Neptune are so far away from the sun that they are colder than anything that we know on earth. It is always very, very cold on these planets.

For a long time people have been very much interested in Mars. They think that there may be living things on it. With their giant telescopes scientists have studied Mars. They have seen great lines that look like ditches or canals. No one is sure what these lines really are. People or the kind of animals we know on earth probably could not live on Mars.

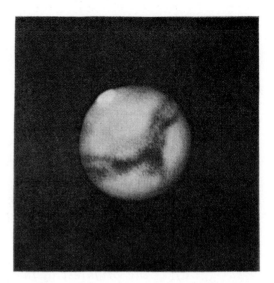

The picture on the left shows a huge telescope. The other picture shows what Mars looks like when seen through a telescope like this.

Perhaps some day scientists will find that there are living things on Mars. This planet seems to have some kind of air, so that living things might be able to stay alive on it. Mars has seasons. At certain times, parts of the planet look green. Some scientists believe that there may be some kinds of plants growing on Mars. But no one has been able to prove that this is true. Other scientists think there are probably no living things on Mars.

1. *Why is it very cold on Pluto and Neptune?*
2. *Why do some people believe that one of the planets besides the earth may have living things on it?*
3. *What two materials must a planet have before it can have living things on it?*

What are shooting stars?

As YOU WATCH the stars, the planets, and the moon, you may see something else in the sky. You may be looking at the Big Dipper or Cassiopeia when suddenly a bright flash shoots across the sky and disappears. It looks like a giant skyrocket though it seems to be far away. You probably say, "Oh! Look at the shooting star."

We call them "shooting stars" or "falling stars," but they are not really stars. They are solid objects traveling through the sky. Whenever the moving earth comes near them, they rush toward the earth. When they reach the ocean of air around the earth, they start glowing. Then we can see them. Scientists call a shooting star a *meteor*.

Meteors travel toward the earth at great speed. They give off light just as any very hot thing does. We look up into the sky and see a bright flash.

As we watch, this light disappears. Do you know what has happened? The meteor has burned up, or perhaps it has hit the earth somewhere. The part of the meteor that falls to the earth is called a *meteorite*. The picture on this page shows a meteor.

If the meteorite is very large, it may go deep into the earth. But most meteors break into little pieces or burn up before they strike the earth. Some meteorites are made of rock, and some are made of iron. Others are made of a mixture of iron and rock.

1. *How are shooting stars different from real stars?*
2. *What are meteors made of?*
3. *When a meteor disappears, what becomes of it?*
4. *Have any shooting stars ever fallen near where you live?*

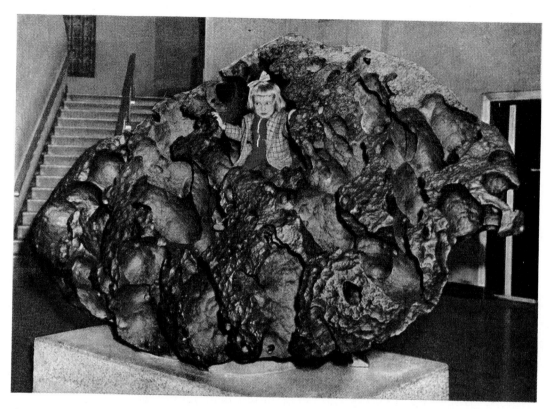

*This large meteorite that fell in the state of Oregon is made of iron and other metals.
Most meteorites are much smaller than this one.*

QUESTIONS TO ANSWER

---

1. How do scientists learn new things about the sun, moon, stars, and planets?

2. Which of the things you can see in the sky

   a) is most like the earth?

   b) seem to change their shapes?

   c) give the earth light?

   d) gives the moon light?

   e) warms the earth?

   f) travel around the sun?

3. Why is it important to know about the North Star?

4. Tell what you have learned about each of these: Venus, The Big Dipper, Mars, Betelgeuse, reflect, the moon, Pluto.

5. How did people first happen to think of stars as being in groups?

6. Why is moonlight not so bright as sunlight?

7. Why do we not see the stars in the daytime?

8. If you were lost at night, how could you use the stars to help you find your way home?

1. Look at the full moon with field glasses and see if you can find plains, valleys, and mountains on it.

2. Read some stories about constellations that are not given in this book.

3. Make a chart showing the pictures of the constellations you can find as you face north.

4. Make a chart showing the pictures of the constellations you can find as you face south.

5. Keep a record on a calendar of the different shapes of the moon as you watch it for a month.

6. Learn to find Mars, Venus, Jupiter, and Saturn during the months when they can be seen.

7. Look at the stars and try to find ones that have different colors.

8. Look for pictures of meteorites.

9. Use different ways to show the constellations you know. Here are two ways you can try.

a) Get a large piece of blue cardboard. Cut holes in the positions of the stars in each constellation. Put Christmas-tree lights in the holes.

b) Cut holes in blue paper to show the positions of the stars in each constellation. Slip the paper into the open end of a box. Then hold an electric-light bulb or flashlight inside the box.

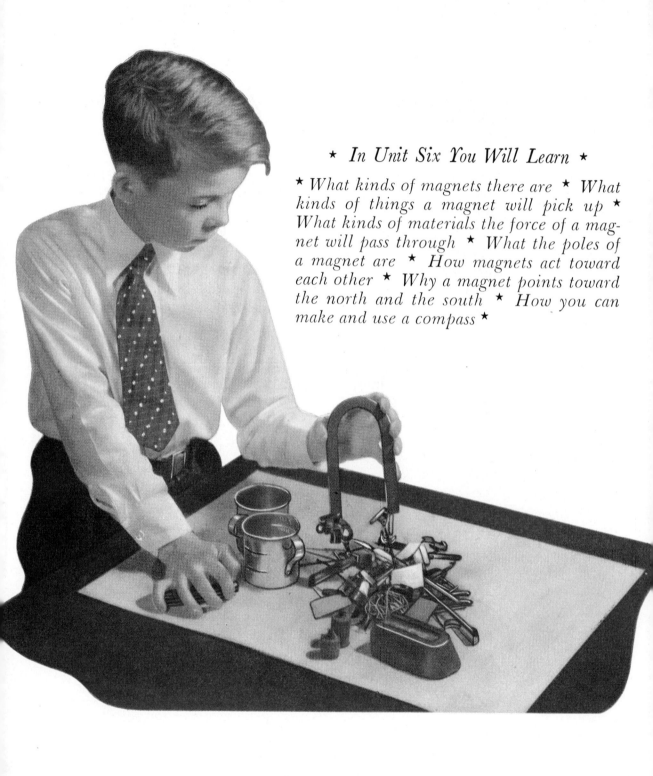

★ *What kinds of magnets there are* ★ *What kinds of things a magnet will pick up* ★ *What kinds of materials the force of a magnet will pass through* ★ *What the poles of a magnet are* ★ *How magnets act toward each other* ★ *Why a magnet points toward the north and the south* ★ *How you can make and use a compass* ★

★ UNIT 6 ★

What Can Magnets Do?

ONE DAY BILLY was having fun with a toy he had made. You can make the same toy if you do what he did. First, he put a straight steel bar called a *magnet* near the front of a small wooden boat. He tied the magnet to the boat so that it could not come off. Then he set the boat in a tub of water. The toy was ready for use.

Billy picked up another straight steel bar like the one on the boat. This bar was a magnet, too. He held one end of it close to the front end of the magnet on the boat. Like magic, the boat moved toward his hand! Billy pulled his hand away slowly, and the boat followed. He made it sail all around the tub of water.

"I wonder what will happen if I hold the other end of this magnet near the front of the boat," Billy said to himself. "I'll try it and see."

Do you know what happened this time? Instead of moving toward his hand, the boat moved away!

"That's funny," Billy thought. "This end pushes, and the other end pulls. The ends of this magnet must be different."

Do you think he was right?

In this unit you will learn several very important things about magnets. As you study magnets, you will understand how one end of the magnet pulled the boat and the other end pushed it. You will find out other interesting things about magnets, too.

139

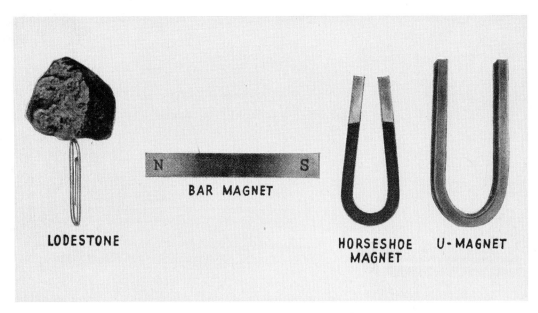

LODESTONE

N   S

BAR MAGNET

HORSESHOE MAGNET   U-MAGNET

What kinds of magnets are there?

NOT ALL MAGNETS are shaped like the ones Billy used. In the picture you can see some other kinds of magnets, too. What are the names of the others?

The magnets in the picture are made of iron or steel. Steel is a metal that is almost all iron. A few years ago all magnets were made of iron or steel. Then scientists discovered a new kind of magnet. This new magnet has in it three other metals besides iron. The metals are aluminum, nickel, and cobalt. This magnet gets its name *alnico* from the first two letters in each of those three words. An alnico magnet is very strong. It will pick up a piece of iron or steel many times as heavy as itself.

There is another kind of magnet. It is found in the ground, and you would never guess that it is a magnet. It looks like a rusty piece of rock, and it is called *lodestone*. Lodestone is a kind of rock that has iron in it. So it is a magnet, too.

No one knows who first discovered lodestone. Different stories are told about how it was found. One old story tells about a young shepherd named Magnes. While he was watching his sheep one day, he set his shepherd's staff down on a rock. The wooden staff had an iron tip on the bottom. When he tried to pick up his staff, the iron tip stuck fast to the rock. He had to pull very hard to get it away. He was so puzzled by what had happened that he told his friends about it. They called the rock a magnet from Magnes, the shepherd's name.

What kinds of things will a magnet pick up?

A MAGNET HAS no fingers, yet it can pick things up. Sometimes it can pick them up even better than you can with both hands. A magnet cannot think, yet it will pick up only certain kinds of things. And it never makes a mistake in the kinds of things it picks up.

You can find out what kinds of things a magnet will pick up by doing an experiment. Be sure to follow the directions carefully. If you are not careful when you do an experiment, you may make mistakes and not get the right answer.

Get as many of these things as you can: tacks, nails, needles, pins, a cop-

This small magnet is an alnico magnet.

per penny, a brass key, a rubber band, an eraser, pen points, paper clips, scraps of paper, bits of cardboard, pieces of iron, steel, wood, and chalk, some sand, something made of glass, and a silver dime. Also get some iron filings. These are tiny bits of iron that have been rubbed off by using a file on iron.

Now get a magnet and see what things it will pick up. Make a list of all the things that the magnet picked up. Make another list of the things the magnet did not pick up. Did it pick up the tacks, nails, needles, pins, pen points, iron filings, and paper clips? Did it pick up the copper penny, the brass key, or the silver dime? The rubber band or the eraser? Paper or cardboard? Wood or chalk? Sand or glass?

Look at the list of things the magnet picked up. All the things in the list are made of metal. But the magnet did not pick up everything made of metal. It did not pick up the copper penny, the brass key, or the silver dime. If any of the pins or tacks were made of brass, the magnet did not pick them up.

Now look carefully at the list again. Do you see how all the things that the magnet picked up are alike in one way? They all have iron or steel in

The man is using a rotating magnetic tube to pick up scraps of iron and steel from the floor. Then the scraps can be used again.

them. As you know, steel is almost all iron. We call iron and steel *magnetic* materials, because a magnet will pick up things made of them. Iron and steel are the commonest magnetic materials. A magnet will pick up only things made of iron, steel, and a few other magnetic materials such as nickel and cobalt.

You found that a magnet will not pick up things made of copper, brass, rubber, paper, chalk, sand, wood, cardboard, or glass. All of these are called *non-magnetic* materials. Most materials are non-magnetic.

Did you notice that the magnet pulled things made of iron or steel toward it and then held them? When you wanted to take one of them off, you had to pull harder than the magnet was pulling. You could feel the pull of the magnet. This pull that the magnet has is called its *force*. We say, "A magnet *attracts* iron and steel." When we say this, we mean that a magnet pulls iron and steel toward it.

You probably found that the magnet does not have to touch a small piece of iron or steel to attract it. When you bring a magnet near a small piece of iron or steel, the piece jumps to the magnet. The force of the magnet makes the iron and steel move toward it.

Can you think of an experiment to show how far a magnet can attract a piece of iron? The boy in the picture on page 142 is doing one. He is slowly moving the magnet closer to the nail. Will the nail roll to the magnet? Try it and see. Use different kinds of magnets and find out which one has the most force. Also try different sizes of magnets.

---

1. *Why should you be careful in following the directions for doing an experiment?*
2. *How can you find out whether a thing is made of magnetic material or non-magnetic material?*
3. *How do you know that a magnet has force?*
4. *What kinds of materials will a magnet attract?*
5. *Does a magnet have to touch a piece of iron to attract it? How do you know?*

What kinds of materials will the force of a magnet pass through?

YOU HAVE LEARNED that magnets attract iron and steel. But what can a magnet do to a tin can? Get a tin can and find out. Did it pick up the tin can just as it did the iron nails and steel pins? Do you think that a magnet can attract tin?

You can find out by testing a used tube of toothpaste with a magnet. The tube is made of tin. The magnet does not attract the tube. Then how does a magnet pick up a tin can?

Here is an experiment to help you understand why the magnet picked up the tin can. Lay a piece of window glass on some books, as shown in the picture. Put some iron nails on the glass. Then hold a magnet against the glass under the nails. Move the magnet around. What happens to the nails? Does the force of the magnet pass through the glass?

Tin cans and most of the other things we call "tin" are made of thin steel with a coating of tin over them. A magnet will not attract tin, but the force of the magnet goes through the tin and attracts the steel in the can. The force of the magnet will go through the paper label on the outside of the tin can, too. Perhaps you can think of an experiment to show that the force of a magnet will go through paper, cardboard, thin wood, cloth, and other non-magnetic materials.

You cannot see this strange force that a magnet has, but you can see what it does and you can feel its pull. You have learned two things about it.

1. A magnet will attract iron and steel.

2. The force of a magnet will pass through many materials.

What are the poles of a magnet?

THERE IS ANOTHER important thing to learn about the force of a magnet. Get some iron tacks and some steel paper clips. How can you tell they are made of iron and steel? Hold a bar magnet in one hand and try to hang the tacks from the magnet. Begin at one end and work along the magnet toward the other end. Which parts of the magnet hold the most tacks? Are there more tacks near the ends or near the center? Where is the force of the magnet strongest? Try the experiment again but use paper clips instead of tacks this time.

Now do another experiment. Spread some iron filings evenly over the bottom of a box. Then lay the bar magnet on the filings and roll it over them. Pick up the magnet. Where do most of the filings stick to the magnet? Try this experiment with a horseshoe magnet and also with a U-magnet.

If you did the experiments carefully, you found that the force of a magnet is strongest near its ends. These ends of a magnet are called its *poles*. One end is called the *north pole*, and the other end is called the *south pole*. As you know, magnets come in different shapes and sizes. But every magnet has a north pole and a south pole. The end marked *N* is the north pole, or *N pole*. The end marked *S* is the south pole, or *S pole*. On some magnets the poles are not marked N and S. On others only the north pole is marked.

Now let us see if we can find out why the poles of a magnet are called north and south. Get a bar magnet whose poles are marked N and S. Tie a piece of string tightly around the middle of the magnet. Then hang the magnet from a wooden stand, as shown in the picture. Why do you

think this stand should not be made of iron or steel?

When you hang the magnet up, be sure that it can swing around easily. Also be sure that there are no other magnets or magnetic materials near. The hanging magnet will swing back and forth for a time and then stop. When it stops swinging, notice in what direction the north pole points. Do you see why it is marked N? Also notice in what direction the south pole points. Do you see why it is marked S? Try the experiment again. Use other magnets, too.

The experiment shows why the poles of a magnet are called north and south. One pole of a magnet points toward the north. It is called the north pole, the N pole, or the north-pointing pole. The other pole of a magnet points toward the south. It is called the south pole, the S pole, or the south-pointing pole.

---

1. *Draw pictures of three shapes of magnets. On each magnet put an X in the places where the force is strongest.*
2. *Where are the poles of a magnet?*
3. *Why must you be sure that there are no magnetic materials near the hanging magnet?*

How do magnets act toward each other?

YOU REMEMBER what happened when Billy brought an end of one magnet near the front end of the magnet on his boat. First, the magnet in his hand pulled on the magnet in the boat. And the boat moved toward his hand. Then he turned the magnet in his hand around and brought the other end near the front end of the magnet in the boat. This time the magnet in his hand pushed on the magnet in the boat, and the boat moved away from his hand. Let us see why the boat was first pulled and then pushed.

Here is a way to find out. You can see what happens when one magnet is brought near another. Get two bar magnets with their poles marked N and S. Hang one bar magnet from the wooden stand that you used before. Pick up the other bar magnet and bring its N pole near the N pole of the hanging magnet. What happens? Now bring the S pole of the magnet in your hand near the S pole of the hanging magnet. What happens this time?

You found that when the N poles of two magnets are brought near each other, they push each other away. Or you can say that one N pole pushes another N pole away. You also found that when the S poles of two magnets are brought near each other, they push each other away. You can say that one S pole pushes another S pole away.

Two N poles are of the same kind. So are two S poles. The experiment shows that when two poles of the same kind come close to each other, they push each other away. Two poles of the same kind are called *like* poles. Like poles of magnets push each other away. A scientist says, "Like poles of magnets *repel* each other." Repel means push away.

Perhaps you can guess what will happen when you bring the N pole of a magnet in your hand near the S pole of the hanging magnet. Try it and see. Then hold the S pole of the magnet in your hand near the N pole of the hanging magnet. What happens this time?

You found that the N pole of one magnet and the S pole of the other magnet pull toward each other. These poles are not alike. One is an N pole, and the other is an S pole. We call these *unlike* poles. We say, "Unlike poles *attract* each other."

From the experiments, we can give two rules about how the poles of magnets act toward each other.

1. *Like* poles of magnets *repel* each other.

2. *Unlike* poles of magnets *attract* each other.

Scientists have found that magnets always follow these rules. An N pole always repels another N pole, and an S pole always repels another S pole. Also, an N pole and an S pole always attract each other.

You can show that these rules are true in other ways. Try to pick up one bar magnet with another. First, lay one bar magnet on the other with like poles next to each other. What happens? Then turn one magnet so that unlike poles are touching. What happens this time? Try this again with two horseshoe magnets and with two U-magnets.

Suppose you have a magnet whose poles are not marked. How can you find which is the N pole and which is the S pole? Get a U-magnet that is not marked and a bar magnet that is marked. Touch one end of the U-magnet with the S pole of the bar magnet. If the poles of the two magnets attract each other, what does this tell you about that pole of the U-magnet? If they repel each other, which pole of the U-magnet did the S pole of the bar magnet push away? Then touch the other pole of the U-magnet with the S pole of the bar magnet. Do these poles of the magnets attract each other or repel each other?

If you remember the two rules about how the poles of magnets always act toward each other, you know that unlike poles attract each other and that like poles repel each other. So when you find the pole of the U-magnet that pulls the S pole of the bar magnet, you have found the N pole of the U-magnet. With a piece of chalk, mark a large N on this pole. Then mark the other end of the U-magnet with a large S. Could you now use the U-magnet to find the N and S poles of another magnet?

---

1. *Write on the board the two rules about how the poles of magnets always act toward each other. Then use two magnets to show that you have written the rules correctly.*
2. *If only one pole of a magnet is marked, can you use it to find the N pole and the S pole of an unmarked magnet? Why?*
3. *The N pole of a magnet attracts both ends of an iron bar. Is the iron bar a magnet? How do you know?*
4. *The S pole of a magnet repels one end of an iron bar but attracts the other end. Is the iron bar a magnet? How do you know?*
5. *What do you think will happen if you bring the N pole of a bar magnet near the middle of another bar magnet? Try it and see.*

Why will a magnet point toward the north and the south?

You know that the N pole of a hanging bar magnet points toward the north. That is why it is called the N pole, or north-pointing pole. You also know that the S pole of a hanging bar magnet points toward the south. That is why it is called the S pole, or south-pointing pole. But do you know why the poles of a magnet always point as they do? Let us see if we can find out.

First, it will be a good idea to make a list of three important things you have learned about magnets.

1. Every magnet has two poles, an N pole and an S pole.
2. Like poles of magnets repel each other.
3. Unlike poles of magnets attract each other.

You can use these three things to help explain why a hanging bar magnet points toward the north and the south. But you must also know one more thing. The earth itself acts like a huge magnet. Maybe that is hard for you to believe, but scientists have found that it is true.

The earth is a huge ball that acts like a magnet. And like all magnets, it has two poles. These are called the earth's *magnetic poles.* One pole is in the far north, and the other pole is in the far south. The one in the far north seems to attract the north-pointing pole, and the one in the far south seems to attract the south-pointing pole.

You can probably guess that a great magnet like the earth must be very strong. Its force reaches far out from its poles. Its force is strong enough to pull or push on the poles of a hanging magnet that is thousands of miles away from the earth's magnetic poles.

That is why a hanging magnet will swing back and forth until it points toward the north and the south. When it points in those directions, it stops swinging.

No matter where a hanging magnet is on earth, the magnetic poles of the earth will attract and repel the poles of the magnet.

How can you make a compass?

A *compass* is used to tell direction on the earth. It makes use of what you have learned about mag- nets. You can easily make a compass yourself, and then you can see how it works. All you need are a marked

Bobby is making his knife into a magnet. How is he doing it? How is he showing that his knife really has become a magnet?

magnet, a steel needle, a flat piece of cork, a knife, and a dish of water. Be sure that the dish is made of glass or china. A compass will not swing around freely in an iron pan. Here are the directions for making a compass. It will look like the picture on this page.

First, make the steel needle into a magnet by rubbing it on one end of the magnet. We call this *magnetizing* the needle. Magnetize means make into a magnet. Rub the needle from the center of a magnet toward one pole. Keep rubbing the needle this one way only—from the center of the magnet to the pole. Do not rub it back and forth.

When the needle is magnetized, test its ends with the S pole of the magnet.

The N pole of the needle will be attracted by the S pole of the magnet. Remember which end of the magnetized needle is the N pole.

Now cut a tiny groove across the cork. Lay the needle in the groove. Then float the cork and the needle in the dish of water. Set them in the water carefully so that the cork does not touch the sides of the dish. The cork must be near the center of the dish so that it is free to turn around. Be sure that there are no magnets or magnetic materials near the dish.

If you followed the directions carefully, the cork will turn until the needle points toward the north and the south. It will act just like the hanging bar magnet. The N pole of the needle will point toward the

The first compasses probably looked something like the one you made.

earth's magnetic pole in the north, and the S pole of the needle will point toward the earth's magnetic pole in the south.

No one knows who made the first compass or when it was made. Long, long ago sailors learned to rub an iron needle on a lodestone. This magnetized the needle. Then they floated the needle on a small piece of wood in a pan of water. The wood turned until the magnetized needle pointed toward the north and the south. Then the sailors could use it to tell directions. Lodestone got its name because it was used to make compasses. Lodestone means leading stone.

The compass is one of the most important inventions ever made. You cannot see the North Star in the daytime or on a cloudy night. You cannot see the sun at night or on a cloudy day. But day or night, in clear or cloudy weather, the needle of a compass points toward the north and the south. No wonder ships and airplanes carry compasses!

With a compass, sailors can guide their ships across the ocean when they are far from land. A compass helps an aviator steer an airplane high above the ground or out over the sea. Explorers used compasses to find new lands. A compass showed Christopher Columbus the way across the Atlantic Ocean to the new world of America. Hunters and trappers use compasses as they tramp through thick woods. So do explorers who go on long travels through strange lands. Think of how many safe journeys have been made with the help of a compass!

---

1. *Why must a compass needle turn easily?*
2. *How can you make a compass?*
3. *What kinds of people use compasses?*
4. *Why is a compass so useful?*
5. *What will happen if a magnet is brought near a compass?*

How can you use a compass?

THE COMPASS that sailors, aviators, explorers, and others now use is not so simple as the one you made. But it works in the same way. Look at the compass on page 152. It has a small needle that can turn easily. The needle is a magnet.

Now look at the card under the needle. Do you see the printed letters that stand for the directions? N is for north, E for east, S for south, and W for west. Notice that halfway between N and E are the letters NE. They stand for the direction called northeast. Find southeast. Also find southwest and northwest.

The end of the compass needle that points toward the north is marked in some special way. On small compasses this end is usually colored blue, black, or silver. You can easily tell which end of the needle points toward the north by its color.

If you have a compass with a colored needle, this is the way to use it. Hold the compass flat in the palm of your hand or set it on a table so that it will be level. When the needle stops swinging, the end of the needle that is colored will point toward the north.

Now turn the case of the compass around so that the letter N is just under the colored end of the needle.

This end of the needle points toward the north. The other end will point toward the south. So you can easily find the other directions from the letters on the compass card.

Which way will south be? You know that it is directly opposite to north. When you face north, east is toward your right and west toward your left. South is at your back. Now use your compass to do these things.

1. Walk ten steps east.
2. Point toward the south.
3. Face northwest.
4. Face southwest.
5. Find what direction the front of your school faces.
6. Find the direction of your home from the school.

You learned that the N pole of a compass needle points toward the magnetic pole in the north. Look at the map on page 154 and find where this pole is. Do you see that it is not at the same spot on the earth as the *geographic* North Pole? The geographic North Pole is at one end of the earth's axis. The magnetic pole in the north is over a thousand miles south of the geographic North Pole! And the magnetic pole in the south is over a thousand miles north of the geographic South Pole! Of course, the compass needle points

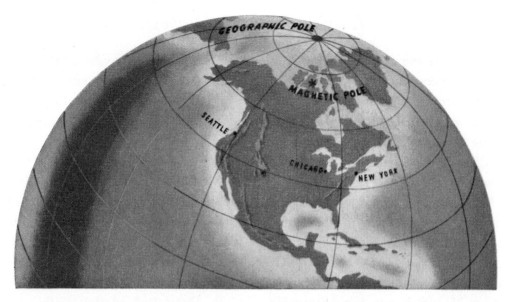

toward the magnetic poles. You can see why at most places on the earth the compass does not point exactly to the geographic North Pole. But it points so close to north that we can use it to find directions.

---

1. *Write down the most important things you have learned about a compass.*
2. *Where would the magnetic poles have to be to make compass needles point exactly north and south everywhere on earth?*

QUESTIONS TO ANSWER

1. How could a magnetic tack hammer keep you from hitting your fingers if you were driving tacks?

2. A story was once told of a thief who stole silver and gold coins from people's pockets with a magnet. Do you believe the story? Why?

3. Find out whether a compass points exactly north in your locality or whether it points east or west of north. Explain why knowing this would help you find directions with a compass.

4. Bud and Jimmy were doing a science experiment. They were trying to find out if a magnet would pick up pins. Bud tried four pins that were lying on the science table. The magnet picked all of them up. Bud said, "Magnets will always pick up pins."

Jimmy found some other pins and tried to pick them up with a magnet.

He discovered that the magnet would not pick up some of these pins. Jimmy said, "Magnets will not pick up all pins. They will pick up only those that are made of iron or steel."

Which of the boys was the better thinker? Why do you think so?

If the two boys were telling you things they had found out about magnets, which boy would you believe?

THINGS TO DO

1. Find out if these things are true by doing some experiments with magnets.

   a) Some magnets are stronger than others.
   b) A magnet's force will pass through a piece of leather.
   c) A nail is itself a magnet when it is touching a magnet.
   d) A magnet can be used to pick iron filings out of sand.

2. Find out whether the force of a magnet will pass through iron and steel.

3. Try to use a compass to find out which of two magnets is stronger.

4. Make a magnetic theater. Use a cardboard box for the toy stage. Cut figures of the actors out of cardboard and fasten paper clips or tacks to their feet. Move the actors by moving a magnet under the stage.

5. Make a magnetic fish pond. Cut out little paper fish and fasten a paper clip to each. Put these in a box. Tie a magnet to a pole and then see who can catch the most fish.

6. Find out what an electromagnet is and how it works.

★ *In Unit Seven You Will Learn* ★

★ *What you can do to keep your body well* ★
★ *How food helps you* ★ *Why you need exercise and rest* ★
★ *How the right clothes help keep you healthy* ★
★ *How you can keep from catching diseases* ★
★ *How you can keep from having accidents* ★

★ UNIT 7 ★

How Can You Keep Well?

"IT'S RUNNING so smoothly you can hardly hear the engine going," said Jack to his father as their automobile moved down the street.

"I just had it tuned up," said Jack's father. "The man at the garage changed the oil and greased everything thoroughly. He tightened some of the parts and put air in the tires. He says the car's in apple-pie order."

When all of the parts of an automobile are doing their work properly, the car runs along smoothly. But when a tire blows out—*Bang*—there is trouble. Or if there is water in the gasoline—*Chug*—the car stops. Or if some part breaks or does not work as it should—*Knock*—the driver begins to wonder what the trouble is and where the nearest garage or filling station is.

Your body is somewhat like an automobile. You know that all of the parts of your body work together so that you can do many different things. Before you read this unit, think how a well body is like a smooth-running automobile and how a sick body is like a broken-down automobile.

When you are well, you seldom think about your body. It runs along without much attention from you. You wake up in the morning, and you feel rested. Your mother says, "Good morning, how are you feeling?" And you say, "I feel fine. What are we having for breakfast?" You are full of pep, and you are hungry. You eat your breakfast and are off to school. You work, play, and enjoy yourself. Your body is running as smoothly as a new automobile.

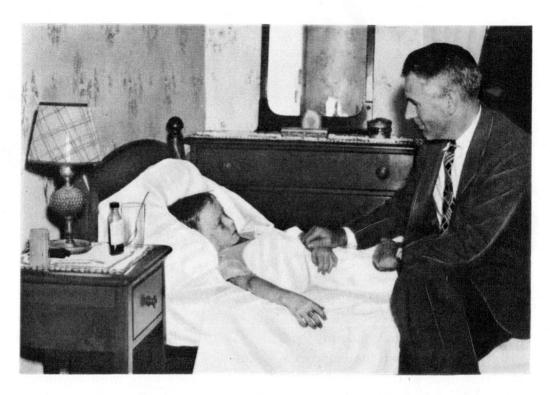

How do you feel when you are sick?

BUT SOMETIMES things are different. You have a headache. You feel chilly even when everyone else feels warm enough. Or you feel so hot that you think you are roasting when everyone else feels comfortable. You sneeze and you cough. Your mother says, "I'm afraid you are coming down with a cold. You had better stay home today."

Or perhaps you have a headache and a sore throat. You look so sick that your mother says, "I think we should ask the doctor to stop in and take a look at you." So the doctor comes. He says to you, "Tell me how you feel." And you say, "I feel terrible." Then he wants you to tell him where you feel bad or what part of you hurts or anything else about you that feels queer.

After you tell him how you feel, he may say, "Well, I think I'd better take your temperature." He puts his thermometer under your tongue, and you cannot talk for a few minutes. While he is waiting for the thermometer to tell your temperature, he puts his fingers on your wrist and counts your heartbeats!

There is a blood vessel in your wrist. Every time your heart beats, it pushes your blood through this blood vessel and makes a beat. So the doctor can tell how your heart is behaving by counting these beats. He can tell whether it is beating too fast or too slow. At your age it should beat about ninety times a minute. As you grow older, your heart will beat fewer times a minute.

After a few minutes the doctor takes his thermometer out of your mouth and reads it. It should read about 98.6 degrees. If it reads much higher than this, he is sure that you have a *fever*. He knows that something is surely the matter with you. Then he may say, "Let me look at your chest." He takes a look. Probably he calls your mother and says, "Look at this." She looks and sees that there are several tiny red spots. Then the doctor says, "This child has measles!" So you go to bed for a few days until you feel better.

The fever, the headache, the sore throat, and the red spots are signs that help the doctor find out what is the matter with you. Signs like these are called *symptoms*. When you tell the doctor your symptoms, you are helping him find out what is wrong with you. The sooner the doctor learns your symptoms, the sooner he can help you get well.

Tommy is having his eyes tested at school. Then his teacher will tell his parents if he needs to go to an eye doctor.

That is why it is wise to call a doctor when you feel sick. Sometimes people wait too long before they call a doctor. Then he may have a very hard time helping them get well. Wise people have learned that it pays to ask advice of a doctor before they get very sick.

Many schools have doctors and nurses to examine girls and boys and help them when they are sick. These doctors and nurses are anxious to help you get well, and they are also anxious to keep you from getting sick. It is much easier to do things that will keep you from getting sick than it is to cure you after you are sick.

Your school nurse and doctor and your family doctor will be glad to know that you are learning how to keep well. Talk to them about what you learn or ask them to help your class by talking to you about keeping well.

---

1. *Why should you call a doctor if you are sick?*
2. *Why do you think you should tell your doctor where you have pain or how you feel queer if you are sick?*
3. *What does* symptom *mean? What symptoms do you have when you have a cold?*
4. *Suppose you were sick and had several symptoms. Would you take a medicine just because an advertisement said it would cure these symptoms?*
5. *Why do you think that people should see a doctor once each year even if they are not sick?*

How can you help keep your body well?

NO GIRL OR BOY or man or woman likes to be ill. Sometimes when you get sick, there is nothing you could have done to keep well. But very often if you had taken better care of yourself, you would not have been sick at all. Your body needs good care even more than an automobile does. You cannot buy a new body every few years. You know, of course, that some automobiles run for years and years without any breakdowns at all. Usually this is because the owners take good care of them. Girls and boys can learn how to take care of their bodies in the same way. Let us see how.

You have already learned how important your heart is to your body. It pumps the blood that carries food to all parts of your body. The blood carries oxygen to all of the parts, too. Without a good heart, you are about as well off as an automobile without a good pump to feed gasoline into the engine.

Be careful not to overwork your heart. Whenever you exercise, your heart beats faster and pumps the blood faster. That is a very good thing if you are careful not to exercise too hard or too long. Here is a picture of a girl skipping rope. She is having fun, and her heart is very busy keeping the blood moving inside her. *If* she stops when she gets tired, then **the exercise will be good for her.** *If* she keeps exercising too long and gets too tired, the exercise may be bad for her. She may overwork her heart.

Sometimes after you have been sick, your heart is not so strong as it was before. After an illness your doctor may say to you, "Take it easy for a while. Don't exercise too much."

You remember that your lungs are another important part of your body. The air that you need gets into your body through your lungs. You need to breathe deeply so that air gets down into every one of those little pockets in your lungs.

Having good *posture* is an important way to help your lungs. Having good posture means holding your body correctly. One part of good posture is sitting up straight or standing up straight. When you are sitting or standing straight, you can breathe deeply. When you are all hunched over, your ribs are crowded together. They cannot move out to make room for your lungs to swell with air.

You remember that your teeth chop and grind your food so that your body can use it. Have you done anything today to help your teeth so that they can do their work? You should brush them each morning and evening to keep them clean.

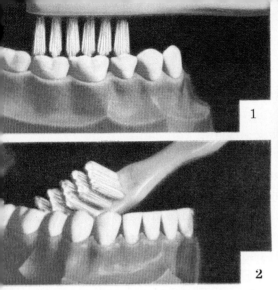
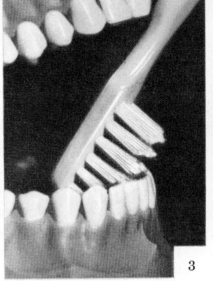

1

2

3   4

And brushing them correctly is very important, too. The pictures on this page will help show you how. Picture 1 shows you how to hold your brush when you brush your large chewing teeth. Always brush the tops of your chewing teeth first. Then brush the outsides of your teeth. Always move the brush straight up and down when you brush the outsides. Brush the inner sides of your teeth last. Pictures 2, 3, and 4 show you how to hold your brush when you brush the insides of your teeth. Always let your brush get dry before you use it again.

You should have your dentist look at your teeth at least twice each year, or as often as your dentist thinks he should. If they need repairing, he can fix them before they are so badly decayed that they have to be pulled.

Foods that are good for growth and health are also good for your teeth. Milk is one of these foods. Drink

plenty of it. Fresh fruits and fresh vegetables help, too. Eat plenty of them. Good, strong teeth will help you keep well.

Your ears must be taken care of, too. Perhaps you think that they are troublesome, because your mother is always telling you to be sure to wash them. A doctor once said, "The only things that should ever go into your ears are a washcloth and your elbow!" Of course, he was partly joking. You cannot reach your ear with your elbow. He meant that you should always keep your ears clean. But he also meant that you should never try to clean them by putting any sharp-pointed things in them.

Keeping your ears clean will help keep them well. But putting anything sharp in them may harm them very much. It may break or pierce the *eardrum*. This eardrum makes it possible for you to hear. The eardrum is a very thin part that is easily broken.

Even a very loud sound may harm it. So you should never shout directly into anyone's ear. Hitting someone on the ear may break this thin eardrum, too. If the eardrum is broken, you may not be able to hear at all. Find the eardrum in the picture on page 84.

Blowing your nose too hard when you have a cold may harm your ears, too! When you have a cold, there are many germs inside your head. If they get inside your ears, they may cause you serious trouble.

Look again at the picture on page 84. You will see that there is an opening between the nose and the ears. If you hold your nose and then try to blow it, air presses back through this opening into your ears. Germs from your nose are blown back into your ears and may cause trouble there.

This girl is reading with a good light.

Your eyes need care, too. Here is a list of important things that you should remember to do or not to do in caring for your eyes. Read the list and try to follow these rules every day.

Safety rules for taking care of your eyes

1. Have a doctor examine your eyes to see if you need glasses.
2. If you wear glasses, be very careful not to break them when you have them on. Be careful not to do anything that might break someone else's glasses.
3. Do not use another person's towel to wipe your face and eyes. It may have germs on it that will get into your eyes.
4. Do not rub your eyes with your fingers. You may rub dirt into them.
5. Do not look straight at the sun.
6. Do not read in light that is very bright and glaring. Light from the sun or from a lamp should not shine directly into your eyes.
7. Do not read in a light that is so dim that you cannot see clearly.

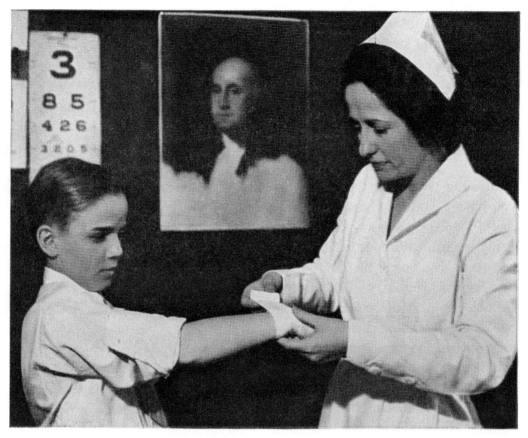

You need to take care of your skin, too. Two things are important to remember about your skin.

1. Keep it clean.

2. Be careful to keep it from getting cut or burned.

A bath with warm water and soap cleans your skin and washes off perspiration. Dust and dirt that fill the pores in your skin are washed away, too. You should take a warm bath or shower at least twice every week. Use plenty of soap. If you want to keep your skin clean and healthy, you must wash it often.

Much of the perspiration soaks into the clothes next to your skin. So the clothes that you wear next to your skin should be changed often and washed in hot, soapy water.

Wash and brush your hair, too, so that it will be clean and so that the skin on your head will be clean. Keep your comb and hairbrush clean, too.

The skin covering of your body keeps germs from getting inside you. The skin does this if you do not cut it or tear it. When your skin is opened at any place on your body, the opening is a door for germs to get in. That is why it is so important for you to keep from cutting your skin or in any way breaking it open.

If you do cut or burn yourself, you should take care of your wound at once even though it is only a scratch. A small cut that has stopped bleeding can be washed and covered with a clean bandage. But if the wound is a bad one, keep it clean by covering it with a bandage that will keep out the dirt until you can see a doctor or a nurse. A doctor or a nurse knows how to take care of a wound to make it heal as quickly as possible.

You have learned that you should take good care of your heart, lungs, teeth, ears, and eyes. And you know that it is important to bathe and change your clothes. You have also learned that germs must be kept from getting into your body through cuts or breaks in your skin. These things and others that you will learn as you study this unit can help you to keep your body well. But there are some other things you can do, too. Do you know what they are?

Just because you know about things that can make you sick, you should not worry about them. Instead, use what you learn to start good habits of keeping well. Try to be happy and cheerful. This is very important at mealtime. If you are cross or angry, the food you eat will not digest well.

You know that your brain is the director of your body. It tells the other parts of the body what to do. But your brain cannot do its work well if you are worried or afraid. Neither can your heart, your stomach, or your intestines. If you are worried or afraid about something, talk to a grown-up about whatever is bothering you. Your mother, father, or teacher can help you get over your worries or fears.

1. Make a set of rules that will help you keep from getting sick. Learn the rules and follow them.
2. Why is it important for each of these parts of your body to be well?
   Heart   Lungs   Ears   Eyes   Teeth   Skin
3. Why should you be careful about blowing your nose hard if you have a cold?
4. How can you tell if your ears, eyes, or teeth need special attention of any kind?
5. Why may even a small burn or a tiny cut in your skin be dangerous?

ENERGY FOODS

BODY-BUILDING FOODS

How does food help you keep well?

TWO VERY IMPORTANT things to remember about keeping your body well are these.

1. Your body needs food.
2. It needs the right kinds of food.

You cannot expect to keep healthy and feel well if you do not eat plenty of good food.

Your body uses the food you eat for several different things. Some of the food gives you pep and energy to play and work. Some helps you grow. Some helps you keep from getting sick. Some helps make blood and the other liquids in your body. Do you see why you should eat many different kinds of foods?

The foods that give you pep and energy are sometimes called *fuel foods* or *energy-giving foods*. When we say that a person has plenty of energy, we mean that he can get lots

of work done in a hurry. Scientists say that energy is the ability to do work. Bread, cereals, potatoes, sugar, and butter are some of the kinds of fuel foods or energy-giving foods. When you eat these foods, your body uses them for fuel very much as an automobile uses gasoline. You need some of these fuel foods for breakfast, for lunch, and for dinner.

Some of the foods that help build a strong body are meat, fish, eggs, and milk. Milk is very good for you because your body uses the materials in milk for building bones and teeth. Every meal that you eat should have some of the *body-building foods* in it.

You have probably heard your parents talk about *vitamins*. These vitamins help protect your body from certain diseases. Foods that contain vitamins are called *protective foods*.

PROTECTIVE FOODS

There are several different kinds of vitamins. Each kind does a different thing for your body. Some foods contain one kind of vitamin. Some contain other kinds. Later on, you will learn more about these vitamins and how they protect your body.

Here are some of the kinds of foods that contain the vitamins you need: green, leafy vegetables, such as lettuce and cabbage; other vegetables, such as celery and tomatoes; fruits, such as oranges, grapefruit, and lemons. Whole-wheat bread and milk also contain vitamins. If you eat plenty of these foods, you will probably get enough vitamins.

Sometimes your doctor may think that you need more vitamins than you are getting in the food you eat. So he will have you take vitamin pills. Some pills give you one kind of vitamin, and some give you another kind. The doctor will know which kind you

need and how many pills you need to take each day.

The water your body needs to make blood and the other liquids comes from the water and the milk you drink. Some of it comes from fruits and vegetables and their juices, too.

When you eat at home, your mother probably plans your meals so that you will get plenty of the right kinds of foods. When you eat in the school cafeteria or are on a vacation trip, you may choose your own food. Then you should use what you have learned to help you. On page 168 is a picture of the food a boy chose for himself for breakfast. Here are the things he selected: orange juice, oatmeal, milk, toast, and an egg. Do you think he made a good choice? Why? How will these foods help keep him well?

On page 168 is also a picture of a girl choosing her lunch at a school cafeteria. She is going to eat scram-

bled eggs, lettuce and tomato salad, a whole-wheat roll, a baked apple, and an oatmeal cookie. She has milk to drink. Is she making a good choice of foods? How do you know?

Some kinds of foods do not help your body in any way. They may even take away your appetite for the foods you need. Coffee and tea are not good for growing children. They do not help you grow. They do not protect you from disease. They do not give you energy.

Candy gives you energy. But it may be harmful for you, too. Do you know why? If you eat candy between meals, you will probably not be hungry at mealtime. The best time to eat candy is soon after you have eaten lunch or dinner.

Eating between meals is usually not a good idea, because it spoils your appetite for your meals. But if you are hungry after school, a glass of milk and a cookie are the best things to eat.

---

1. *Explain why you should eat several different kinds of foods at each meal.*
2. *Why should you drink plenty of milk?*
3. *Do you think it is a good idea to take vitamin pills without asking a doctor if you need them? Why?*
4. *If you went to a cafeteria, how could you choose the right kind of foods?*
5. *Decide what kinds of foods would make a good dinner. List these foods and tell why you chose them.*
6. *Why may eating between meals be bad for you?*

Why do you need exercise and rest?

EXERCISE AND REST both help keep you well. Here are important things every boy and girl needs to remember about exercise. Which ones do you already know? Which ones are new to you? Most important of all, *Which of these rules do you follow?*

1. Do not exercise too hard at first. "Warm up" slowly.

2. Do not exercise too long or too hard. Do not play until you are "dead tired."

3. Do not exercise right after breakfast or lunch or supper.

4. Cool off slowly after you have been playing hard. Do not sit in a draft to cool off fast.

Exercise makes your muscles strong. A boy or girl who skates, swims, plays games, hikes, and takes other kinds of exercise will have stronger muscles than one who does not. Exercise makes you breathe deeply. Breathing deeply gets more air into your lungs and gets this air into all parts of your lungs, too. This helps you keep well.

Rest is just as important for you as exercise. After you have worked and played all day, your body is tired. Some parts of your body get worn out when you exercise. Your body needs time to repair the parts that have been worn out. Boys and girls of your age need lots of sleep. Look

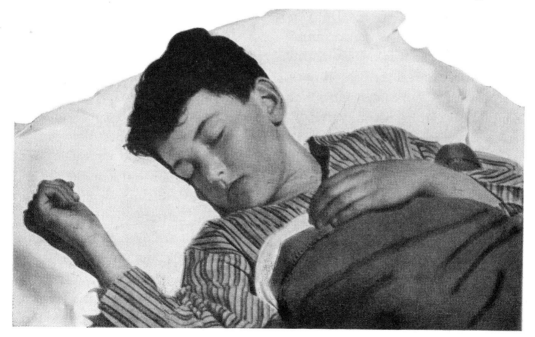

at the chart below and find out how much sleep you should have every night.

Years Old	Hours of Sleep
6-7	12
8-10	11
11-13	10-11

Here are the important things to remember about rest and sleep.

1. Be sure to get enough rest and sleep.

2. Go to bed regularly in time to get the right number of hours of sleep for your age.

3. Sleep in a dark room with the windows partly open to give you plenty of fresh air.

If you use the rules on these pages when you exercise and rest, you are much more likely to keep well than you are if you do not make it a habit to follow them.

---

1. *List the rules that you should follow when you exercise and rest. Try to follow them carefully.*
2. *Why do you need exercise and rest?*

How can the right clothes help you keep healthy?

EVEN THE CLOTHES you wear can help you keep well. Do you know how your clothes can do this? We often say, "That is a very warm coat." But if you feel the coat, it does not feel warm. The coat itself is not warm. Yet it can keep you warm. It keeps you warm by holding in the heat of your body. If you feel your body, you can feel the warmth in it. The coat and other clothes you wear keep this warmth from getting away. So your body is kept warm.

In winter, you need clothes that will keep the heat from getting away from your body. In summer, you need clothes that will let the heat get away. That is why you have some clothes for winter and other clothes for summer. When you are indoors, you do not need so many clothes as you do when you are outdoors. That is why you should take off your heaviest clothes when you come indoors and put them on again when you go out into the cold. Do not sit around indoors with your outdoor clothes on.

It is fun to walk and play in the rain and snow. But it is better for your health if you are dressed for it. Rubbers, raincoats, and overshoes keep you dry. If you go outside in the rain and snow without the right clothes, your clothes soon are wet through.

You feel chilled because the heat from your body gets away easily through wet clothes. When you are chilled, you may easily take cold. Whenever you come in from outdoors and your clothes are wet, you should put dry clothes on at once.

Picture 1 is an X ray of a six-year-old child's feet. The right shows the foot inside the shoe. This child's shoes were always too short for his feet.

Picture 2 is an X ray of a child's foot in two shoes of different sizes. The child's left foot is in the shoe he has outgrown. The shoe on the right foot has been fitted to allow for more space for the toes.

Picture 3 shows a child's foot being measured. The inset picture in the corner is an X ray of a seven-year-old child wearing shoes that fit correctly. Can you see the differences between this picture and the two above?

If you keep on wearing shoes that are too small, your toes may get squeezed out of shape. Tight shoes often cause blisters and other sores on your feet. They are often dangerous as well as very uncomfortable.

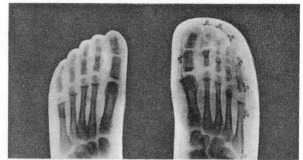

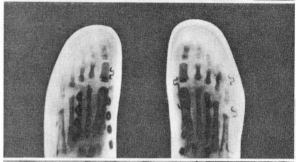

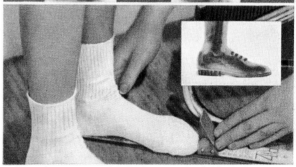

Shoes that are too large may rub up and down and make blisters, too. The next time you get new shoes, be sure that they fit you well.

---

1. *Explain how your coat keeps you warm.*
2. *What kinds of clothes should you wear for different kinds of weather? Explain why you should wear those kinds of clothes.*
3. *Are you wearing the right kind of clothes today? Explain your answer.*

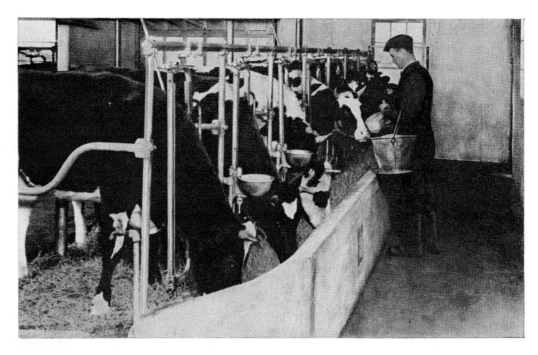

Farmers who sell milk should keep their cow barns as clean as this one.

How can you keep from catching diseases?

GERMS ARE ENEMIES of a well body. In Unit Three you learned that germs are very tiny plants or animals that can make you sick when they get inside your body and grow there. Some kinds of germs cause one disease. Some kinds cause another. Germs can make you sick only if they get inside your body. You have already learned one way in which germs get inside you. They go in through cuts and breaks in your skin. Germs get into your body in other ways, too. Do you know some of these ways?

Germs can get into your body on the food you eat and in the water you drink. You put them in your mouth if you put your dirty fingers in your mouth. They can get in through your nose when you breathe. Germs are spread from people who are sick to people who are well. Can you think of some of the ways you can keep germs from getting into your body?

All food and water that you eat and drink should be clean. Fruits and vegetables should be carefully washed before they are used. Food should be kept covered so that flies will not walk on it. Be sure to buy your food from stores that keep the food clean.

You know that milk is one of the most important foods you need. It is good food for germs, too. That is why you should be sure to drink only clean milk. The people who handle the milk should also be clean. The cows that give the milk should be kept clean, too.

Just to be very sure that there are no disease germs in the milk you drink, look on the label of the bottle and see if the milk is *pasteurized.*

This means that the milk has been heated enough to kill the germs that may be in the milk. It is always safest to drink milk that has been pasteurized.

The germs that cause several serious diseases are carried in water. If you live in the city, your drinking water is probably made safe by the city. If you live in the country, your well water should be tested by the Department of Health every now and then to make sure that it is safe for you to drink.

Sometimes it is better not to share things. Can you tell why this is true?

When you are on a picnic or a camping trip, do not drink water from streams or springs unless they have a sign saying "Safe Drinking Water." It is best to boil water unless you are sure that it is pure. Always use your own cup or glass and do not drink out of cups left in public places. At school be careful not to touch the drinking fountains with your mouth.

Some people have a bad habit of putting their fingers in their mouths. Just think of the number of things your fingers have touched in the last few hours. All of these things may have germs on them. Whenever you bite your fingernails or put your fingers in your mouth, you are helping these germs get into your body. Do not put your fingers into your mouth.

Then you will not help germs get inside of you.

There are many more things to learn about how to keep germs from getting inside of your body to make you sick. There are also many things to learn about how you can help keep disease germs from spreading. There is one important thing you can do. If you have a cold, stay away from school until you are well. Coughing and sneezing spread colds very quickly. If you must cough or sneeze, be sure to cover your nose and mouth with your handkerchief.

Later on, you will learn more about what germs are and how they travel from one place to another. You will also learn what they do inside your body and how your body fights them.

---

1. *Make a list of the ways that germs can get into your body. Then explain what you can do to keep them out.*
2. *How can you be sure that the milk and water you drink are pure? Why do they need to be pure?*
3. *Why should you keep your fingers out of your mouth?*
4. *Tell what things you have learned about each of these.*
   Germs   Coughing   Pasteurizing

How can you keep from having accidents?

EVERY YEAR hundreds and hundreds of boys and girls are hurt at home, on the streets, or at school, where they work and play. That is why you should learn how to play and work so carefully that you will not have an accident. If you read these pages and study the pictures and then remember to do what you have learned, you may be able to keep yourself or someone else from getting hurt.

One picture shows a roller skate that has been left on a stair step. In a few minutes someone may hurry down the stairs and step on the skate. This person may fall and be very badly hurt. Never leave toys or other things in places where someone may fall over them. Never leave your bicycle or wagon in any place where someone may fall over it after dark. Of course, you know that you should not do these things. But do you *remember* not to do them?

Scissors, knives, and other sharp things often cause very bad accidents. Running with scissors in your hand is very dangerous. If you fall, you may get hurt. When you are cutting with a knife, cut *away* from your hand, never *toward* your hand.

Almost every day children are burned because they light matches and set fire to their clothes. Here is a safe rule for you to follow. *Never light a match unless an older person is with you.* Always be very careful with matches.

Bonfires are lots of fun to watch. But they are often very dangerous, too. They can blaze up and set peo-

Is the boy using his bicycle safely? What accidents might happen?

ple's clothes on fire. Boys and girls should never build bonfires unless some grown-up person is with them. If your clothes ever should catch fire, *do not run.* Running will only make the fire burn faster. Cover yourself with a blanket or coat. Or lie down and roll over slowly on the ground.

Drinking anything from a bottle that you find in a medicine cabinet or a cupboard is a dangerous thing to do. Some of the bottles may have poison in them. They may not have labels on them. Never put anything from the medicine cabinet in your mouth unless you know what it is. Then you will be sure never to make a mistake.

You will need to be careful many times when you are on the way to school. If you live in the country and walk to school along a highway, walk on the left side of the road. Then you

can always see an automobile that is coming toward you and can get off the road. A car coming behind you will be on the other side of the road.

In a town or city where you have to cross busy streets, stop and look both ways before crossing. If your school has a Safety Patrol, cross only where the Safety Patrol is helping children across the street. Always obey the Safety Patrol as the boys and girls in the picture are doing. Take time to be safe. Get up early enough so that you do not have to run to school. It is very easy to forget to look both ways when you cross a street if you are in a hurry.

Do you have roller skates or a bicycle? Be sure that you always use them safely. Think of other people on the sidewalk when you are skating so that you do not run into them. Skating in the street is never safe.

Many accidents are caused by bicycles. If you ride in the street, always keep to the right side near the curb. It is never safe to hang on to the back of a truck while you are riding. Riding on the sidewalk is dangerous for people walking there. Always have a bell so that you can warn people quickly. It is safest not to ride a bicycle at night. But if you have to ride at night, be sure to have a light that is in good working order on the front of your bicycle. On the back, have a tail light or a reflector.

You can remember the safety rules for riding bicycles if you make a list of the important things you read on these pages. Then be sure to remember to do the things that will keep you and other people safe.

There are many, many accidents at school because people are not careful. Do not hurry or crowd on the stairs.

You may fall and break an arm or a leg, or you may cause someone else to fall. When there is a fire drill, obey the rules quickly but quietly. Then you and your classmates will get into the habit of leaving the building in an orderly way. If there is a real fire, no one will be hurt because of someone else's carelessness.

When people are drinking at the drinking fountain, do not shove or push anyone's face down against the fountain. You may hurt his teeth or eyes very badly if you do.

Outdoors on the playground there are many things you can do to keep from being hurt. Some schools have a clean-up committee to see that there are no nails or pieces of broken glass or metal that could cut or injure the children. You may find that this is a good idea. Do not ride bicycles on the playground. You may run into

someone and hurt him very badly. When you play on swings, slides, and other playthings, be sure not to hit anyone.

After school, on holidays, and during your vacation, you will be doing many different things. You will have much more fun if you do them safely so that you do not have a serious accident. Of course, it is no fun to spend a lot of your vacation in bed. It is no fun to be unable to do things you had planned just because you were careless. Remember the safety rules that you have learned about using skates and bicycles.

In wintertime, when you want to go coasting, find a safe place to do it. In many towns the police will help you by roping off a hill for coasting. Find out if there is such a hill near you and go coasting there. Always coast on a hill that is safe

from passing cars. Coasting down a hill or driveway that leads to a busy street is a very dangerous thing to do.

Ice skating is fun and good exercise, but be careful on deep ponds. It is safer to skate on a pond that has been made by flooding a shallow place. But if you go to a real pond or a river to skate, be sure that the ice is safe. If there is a hole or spot marked "Danger! Thin Ice!" stay away from it. Being safe is always wiser than trying to be daring.

In the summer, swimming is one of the most healthful sports. But there are some rules that you should remember to follow. Always wait at least two hours after eating before going into the water. You may get cramps if you swim soon after you have eaten. Do not go swimming alone. Go with someone else. Go with an older person who knows how to swim if you are not a good swimmer. Of course, you must be sure to stay in shallow water until you can swim well or unless you have a good swimmer with you. If you can swim well, you will have a great deal of fun. And still more important, being able to swim may save your life sometime.

---

1. *Look at the pictures on pages 175-179. Which ones show you ways to act safely? What accidents can be prevented in these ways?*
2. *What rules for safety should you follow when you do each of these things?*

   Swim   Walk to school   Skate   Ride a bicycle
   Play on the playground   Go coasting
3. *Make a list of rules that tell you how to keep from having accidents at home. Then remember to follow these rules.*

Do you think these boys might have accidents? What do you think might happen?

1. Look at the pictures on these two pages. What accidents could happen to these boys? What safety rules can you think of for each picture?

2. Why should you each have your own comb, brush, toothbrush, towels, and washcloths? How should you take care of these things?

3. Make a list of the foods you eat at your meals during a week. Are you eating some of the right kinds of foods at each meal? If not, tell what you could do to make your meals more healthful.

4. Make a list of five things which you should not do because they are harmful to your body. In what way does each of these things harm your body?

5. Think of some accidents that you have seen or heard about. Answer these questions about the accident.

   a) In what way did the accident happen?

   b) Whose fault was it?

   c) How could it have been prevented?

1. Tell why you think boys and girls should learn about the things that are in this unit.

2. Make a list of everything you can do at home and at school to help keep things clean. Put the list on a large chart to help you remember to do these things.

3. Find out more about good posture. Then do the things that will make your own posture better.

4. Find pictures in magazines and newspapers that show people using their eyes incorrectly. Find pictures that show people using their eyes correctly.

5. Ask your doctor or school nurse to talk to you about how to keep well and how to avoid accidents.

6. Talk with your mother about how she plans your meals so that you will have the correct food.

7. Find pictures of different kinds of foods in magazines and newspapers. Cut the pictures out, paste them on a chart, and then tell what each food does for you.

8. Find out more about how foods are kept fresh and clean at the store and at home. Look for pictures that show some of the ways.

9. Find pictures that show places where accidents may happen. Tell what you could do to keep from having an accident.

10. If you do not already have a Safety Patrol in your school, find out how you can organize one.

★ In Unit Eight You Will Learn ★

★ What happens when animals grow ★ How insects grow ★
★ How amphibians grow ★ How other groups of animals grow ★
★ How plants with seeds begin to grow ★ How plants grow taller ★
★ How the roots of plants grow longer ★ How the stems get thicker ★
★ In what directions the parts of plants grow ★

★ UNIT 8 ★

How Do Animals and Plants Grow?

DO YOU REMEMBER the snowman you talked about in the first unit of this book? You remember that you compared a snowman with a real man and decided that a snowman is not a living thing. One of the reasons you gave for deciding that way was that a snowman cannot grow.

But if you ever made a snowman, you know that you begin by making a little ball of snow in your hands. Then you start rolling it. As you roll the ball, it keeps adding more snow and getting bigger and bigger. This looks as if the snowball is growing.

You know that animals and plants do not get bigger in this way. The snowball gets bigger by just adding more snow on the outside. But a kitten or a dog does not get bigger by just adding milk and meat to the outside of itself. It must eat these foods. Then they are changed and become part of the animal. Plants also need

to use food for growing. All living things grow bigger in this way.

There is another way in which you could tell that a snowman does not grow the way living things grow. The snowball gets bigger and bigger, but it cannot change into a snowman by itself. You have to put on its head and arms and make its face. A snowman cannot change and make new parts by itself as livings things do.

You have probably seen how some living things change as they grow. Perhaps you have had a kitten or a puppy that has grown up into a big cat or dog. Or perhaps you have planted a garden and watched flowers and vegetables grow from the tiny seeds that you put into the ground.

Animals and plants have many different ways of growing. In this unit you will learn about the changes that some kinds of animals and plants make when they grow.

183

This black snake has just molted its skin. A snake may molt its skin several times a year.

What happens when animals grow?

ONE DAY WHILE Nancy was looking at some caterpillars that had been brought to class, she called out, "Come and look at this."

A group of boys and girls gathered around the caterpillar cage. To their surprise, the skin of one of the caterpillars had split open and the caterpillar was coming out! Slowly it crawled out of its skin and stretched itself out on a leaf.

The children had watched one of the most interesting things that happen to a caterpillar while it is growing. Our skin grows larger and larger as we grow, but the skin of a caterpillar does not grow bigger. When a caterpillar gets so big that its skin is too tight, the old skin splits. Out comes a larger caterpillar with a new and larger skin. When a caterpillar sheds its old skin like this, we say that it *molts* its skin.

Some other animals molt, too. Snakes molt their skins several times a year even when they are full-grown. Birds molt their feathers several times a year.

If you have ever found a tadpole in a pond in the spring and kept it where you could watch it grow, you know what happens. After many weeks the animal changes from a wiggling tadpole that lives in the water to a frog or toad that hops about on land.

The frog or toad seems almost to change from one kind of animal into another. Some animals make surprising changes. Other animals just get bigger and bigger without changing very much. Fish and reptiles just grow larger. They do not change in the strange ways that caterpillars and tadpoles change as they grow.

Birds go through some changes as they grow. A baby chick is covered with soft down. It is no larger than your fist, but you can tell that it is a young bird. When it grows up, it is covered with feathers and it has a red comb on top of its head. Some mammals change as they grow, too.

Can you think of other ways in which animals change as they grow? Suppose your teacher wrote this question on the board, "What three very important things happen when animals grow?" How would you answer it?

Here are three things that one class agreed on.

1. Animals get bigger when they grow.

2. Animals may add new parts to themselves when they grow.

3. Some animals change so much while they are growing that they look like different kinds of living things at different times during their lives.

---

1. Read again the sentences numbered 1, 2, and 3 above. Then think of one or two changes in some growing animals to show what each sentence means. Try to think of things that are not told in your book.

2. How have you changed since you were two or three weeks old? Think of all the changes you can.

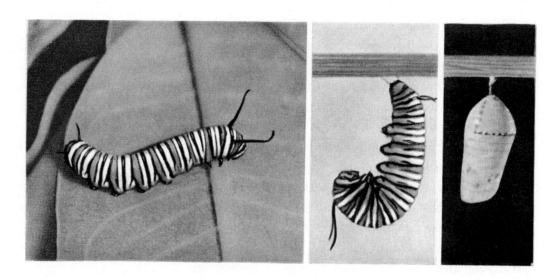

How do insects grow?

OF COURSE, the class was keeping close watch on the caterpillars in the cage. One was a striped caterpillar that Peggy had found on a milkweed plant. Milkweed was the only food that this kind of caterpillar would eat. The pictures on these two pages show you what the striped caterpillar did.

For several days the caterpillar did almost nothing but eat. Peggy had to bring milkweed leaves every day. But one day it stopped eating and crawled up the side of the cage. Then it crawled along the underside of the board that covered the cage. It seemed to be looking for a hiding place. At last, it stopped and began to spin some silky threads that stuck tightly to the board. Then it fastened one end of its body to these

silky threads and let the rest of its body hang down.

The caterpillar hung there for almost a day. The class watched closely, but it was not until the next morning that they saw what had happened. To everyone's surprise, they saw something that was not a caterpillar. There, hanging from the board, was a beautiful green case with gold spots on it.

This case did not look at all like the black and yellow caterpillar. It did not even look alive. It was hard and almost like a shell. It was no longer a caterpillar. It was a *chrysalis*.

"Well, I wonder what's going to happen next," said Nancy, as she looked at the chrysalis. "We will have to watch the green case carefully to find out."

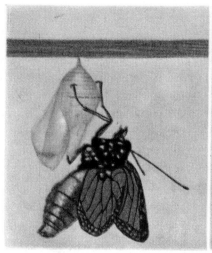

For about two weeks the chrysalis hung there. Slowly the case changed color and became dark brown. Then it began to get so light-colored that the boys and girls could almost see through it.

And at last they saw the most surprising change of all. The case began to split open, and out came an insect. It was a beautiful butterfly.

At first, the wings were wrinkled and folded together. And they looked moist as if they had been wet. After a while the butterfly began to stretch them out and to open and close them. The boys and girls could see that the wings were drying and getting stiff. By the next morning the wings were full-sized, and the butterfly was flying about in the cage.

The butterfly did not grow larger. Soon after it came out of its case, it was as large as it would ever be. Of course, the boys and girls wanted to know the name of this butterfly. It is called the Monarch butterfly.

You have just learned how the Monarch butterfly grows. You have read about three *stages* of its life— the caterpillar stage, the chrysalis stage, and the butterfly stage. But where did the caterpillar come from?

If you look at the leaves of milkweed plants, you may find some little brown or green dots about the size of pinheads. These dots are eggs laid by a Monarch butterfly. The caterpillar that Peggy brought to school had hatched from an egg like one of these. Of course, it was only a tiny thing at first. But it ate and ate and grew and grew. It molted its skin two or three times before it made a chrysalis.

One morning Henry brought a big caterpillar to class. It was almost four

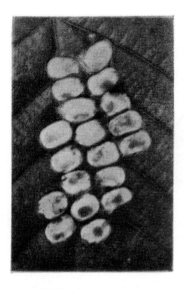

inches long. It was bluish-green with knobs of different colors sticking out from it. Henry put it in the cage for the class to watch.

One day Henry noticed this caterpillar doing something that the caterpillar of the Monarch butterfly had never done. It was moving its head around, and a silk thread was coming from its mouth. As the caterpillar moved its head, it threw the silk around its body. Soon it was covered with so much silk that it could not be seen. The caterpillar was making a *cocoon* for itself.

The cocoon made a warm covering for the caterpillar. This kind of caterpillar takes all winter long to change. And while it is changing, it needs a warm cover. In the cocoon the living caterpillar slowly changes into the head, body, feelers, legs, and wings

of an insect. But it is not a butterfly. It is a *moth*.

Moths are very much like butterflies, but they usually fly at night. They also have heavier bodies than butterflies, and their colors are not so bright as the colors of butterflies. Moths keep their wings out flat when they are resting on something. Butterflies hold their wings straight up and together when they are at rest.

The pictures on these pages show you what this moth looks like and how it grows. It is called a Cecropia moth. It begins life as an egg, just as a butterfly does. And it molts its skin while it is a caterpillar.

The four stages of a butterfly's life and of a moth's life make one of the most interesting stories about how living things grow. First, there is an egg. This hatches into a caterpillar,

which molts as it grows larger. A moth caterpillar spins a cocoon, and a butterfly caterpillar makes a chrysalis. From the chrysalis comes a butterfly, and from the cocoon comes a moth. The butterfly and the moth are both as big as they will ever be as soon as their wings are dry.

Bees, ants, and flies are some of the other insects that have four stages to their lives. Eggs of honeybees hatch in about three days. The bee is then just a tiny wormlike animal. In a few days it spins a thin cocoon. Several days later, the bee hatches into a full-grown bee.

The common housefly takes about eleven days to change from an egg to a full-grown fly. A housefly is like a butterfly. As soon as it has wings, it is as large as it will ever be. A little fly does not grow to be a big fly.

All insects go through changes as they grow up, but they do not all have four stages in their lives as the butterfly and the moth do. Look at the pictures on page 190 to see how some other insects change as they grow.

In late summer and early autumn, the grasshopper lays a little case full of eggs in the ground. In the spring, the eggs hatch out into little grasshoppers. They have small bodies, long legs, and no wings at all. After eating grass for a few days, they molt their skins just as caterpillars do. They molt their skins five times while they are growing. After the fifth time they are full-grown insects with wings. Look at the picture at the top of page 190. This shows the three stages that a grasshopper goes through while it is growing from an egg to a full-grown grasshopper.

GRASSHOPPER

A cricket is another insect that grows up in the way that a grasshopper does. A cricket, too, has only three stages in its life. First, there is the egg. Then there is a young cricket with no wings. After molting several times, the cricket is full-grown and has wings.

1. Put these words in the right order to show how a butterfly grows.
   Chrysalis   Egg   Butterfly   Caterpillar
2. What stages do grasshoppers and crickets go through during their lives?
3. Why does a caterpillar need to molt its skin?
4. Which changes more as it grows, a cat or a butterfly? Tell why you think so.
5. What new parts does a grasshopper add while it is growing?
6. Finish these sentences.
   A butterfly caterpillar makes a _____.
   A moth caterpillar spins a _____.
7. Which grows more rapidly from an egg to full size, a grasshopper or a housefly?

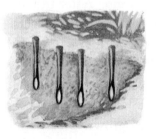

CRICKET

FEELERS

MOTH

FEELERS

BUTTERFLY

Here is another way to tell butterflies from moths. Look at their feelers or antennae. Butterflies have long thin antennae. Moths' antennae look like little feathers.

How do amphibians grow?

EVERY DAY the boys and girls spent much time studying the animals in their aquarium. Fish darted in and out through the plants. Tadpoles swam around with their wiggling tails. The class enjoyed looking at the tadpoles because they could see that the tadpoles were changing. Two little legs had grown out from their bodies. And their tails seemed to be getting shorter, too.

The life story of a frog is just as interesting as the story of an insect's life. In the spring, the mother frog lays her eggs in a pond or quiet stream. She may fasten them to the stem of a water plant or to a dead tree branch in the water, or she may just let them float. She lays hundreds of eggs all together in a kind of jelly, as you see in the picture on page 192.

If you look at one of these eggs, you can easily see a little black dot in it. As the bright spring sun warms the water day after day, the black dot becomes larger. At last, you can see it move. Before long, that black part wiggles loose from the mass of jelly. A tiny tadpole has hatched from the frog egg.

Almost as soon as the tadpole is hatched, little fringes begin to grow

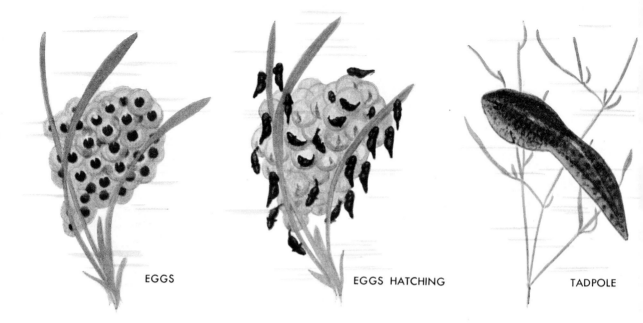

EGGS

EGGS HATCHING

TADPOLE

on each side of its head. These are gills. The tadpole breathes with them just as a fish breathes with its gills. Slowly this little animal grows bigger. In a few weeks it makes another change. Its two hind legs grow out.

The children watched the tadpoles closely. They wanted to see how the tadpoles changed so that they could live on land. The little animals already had two hind legs. Perhaps you think the next change was getting two front legs. But it was not. The tadpoles pushed one front leg out first and then swam around with three legs.

The class knew that another leg was coming, for they could see it folded up under the skin. And then, after a time, out came the other front leg. Now the tadpoles had four legs, and they went swimming around with

their tails wiggling and their legs hanging down.

All this time their tails had been getting shorter and shorter. At last, they were just little stubs. The tadpoles were getting to look more and more like little frogs.

Changes also had been going on inside the bodies of the tadpoles. They were losing their gills, and they were growing lungs. With these lungs they could breathe air on land. One day the class saw one of the little frogs climb slowly out on a block of wood that was floating in the water. There it sat, looking around with its funny little popeyes. The tadpole had become a frog!

Do you think it was now a grown-up frog? Not at all. It was only about an inch and a half long. You know that many frogs are much larger than that.

TADPOLE   TADPOLE   FULL-GROWN FROG

Of course, it grew bigger and bigger as the days and weeks went by. But it did something else while it was growing. It did the same thing that the caterpillar did. It molted its skin, and this is the funny way that it did it. The old skin split down the middle of the back and the middle of the front. It also split along the tops of the four legs. Then the frog wiggled and wiggled to get out. It had to pull its front legs out and its hind legs out. Frogs molt their skins in this way several times while they are growing.

Some kinds of frogs grow to full size much faster than others. And some kinds of frogs are much larger than others. Bullfrogs grow to be great big fellows that weigh two or three pounds. They are tadpoles for more than a year. After that, it

may take them two or three years to grow to full size. But some frogs hatch in the early summer and are full-grown by the time winter comes.

One day while the class was learning all these things about frogs, Nancy said, "Frogs are amphibians, and so are toads. But I never saw a toad in the water."

"I have," said John. "I've seen them in the water in the spring when I was collecting frogs' eggs. But I never saw them in the water any other time."

Toads go to the water only in the spring, and they go then to lay their eggs. Toads' eggs are black. They are laid in long strings of grayish jelly. The picture on the next page shows you some strings of toads' eggs. Perhaps John had seen toads' eggs, but did not know what they were.

Toads' eggs hatch out into little toad tadpoles and then change into little toads in almost the same way that frog tadpoles change into frogs.

---

1. *Here are some of the changes that frogs make while they are growing. Put them in the order in which they happen.*

   Come out of the water   Get hind legs
   Get front legs   Molt their skins

2. *Which is older, a tadpole with hind legs or one with front legs?*
3. *What hatches from a toad egg?*

How do other groups of animals grow?

MAMMALS, BIRDS, reptiles, and fish change while they are growing. But they do not change as amphibians and insects do. They do not change so much that they seem to change from one animal to another. Snakes molt their skins while they are growing, but they do not change their looks. They look like snakes from the moment they are born or hatched. A fish looks like a fish as soon as it hatches.

When you see a baby bird, you cannot always be sure what kind of bird it is. Many kinds of baby birds do not look much like their parents. Have you ever found a nest of baby robins and watched the young birds grow? You knew that they were robins because you saw the mother

feeding them worms. But if you found one of the little birds away from its nest, you might have wondered what kind of bird it was.

Bluejays and robins have no feathers or other covering on their skins when they hatch. They stay in the nest and are sheltered until they have feathers. Robins grow feathers in about eleven days. Even a young robin that has feathers and has left its nest does not yet look exactly like its parents. At first, it has no tail feathers. So it has a hard time flying. Its breast is speckled for a while after its tail feathers grow. It is speckled until the young robin is almost full-grown.

Baby chicks are covered with fluffy down when they hatch. They can run around and get their own food right away. Baby ducks and many other young water birds are also covered with down. They can go into the water to hunt for their own food almost as soon as they hatch. Most of them do not look much like their parents until their feathers begin to grow. The baby Canada geese in the picture on this page will begin to look like their parents when they are about three months old. Then they get the colors and markings that tell you what kind of bird they are.

Kittens and puppies are easy to recognize when they are tiny. You could probably tell what kind of animal most other mammals are even when they are very young. But mammals change, too, as they grow. Some change the markings of their coats. Baby lions have spotted coats like the ones in the picture on page 183. They keep these spots until they are about a year old. Then the spots disappear, and their coats are like those of their parents.

Young deer, or *fawns*, as they are called, are spotted, too. These spots make it very hard to see the fawns among the leaves. When the fawns get their first winter coats, they lose their spots and have coats of the same color as full-grown deer.

Some mammals change more than this when they grow. You probably would not know a baby black bear if you saw a very young one. People do not often see the very young black bears. They are born in the winter and stay with their mother in the den, where she is spending the winter. When the little bears come out in the spring, they are about three months old.

But when the black bears were born, they were only about the size of a squirrel and had almost no hair. Their eyes were closed, and the mother bear had to give them a great deal of care. They did not look much like the bears that you see at the zoo.

Some other mammals have no fur when they are born. Did you ever find a nest of tiny mice or rats? The small, pink, naked animals have to grow and change a great deal before they look like mice.

You yourself have changed very much since you were a month old. If you look at your baby pictures or at the clothes you wore, you will probably think, "I've certainly grown a lot." You are taller, and you weigh more. You have grown stronger. Your muscles are larger. Your bones are larger and stronger. You did not have any teeth when you were a month old. Since then, you have grown one set of teeth, and now you are getting another. As you get older, you keep on growing and changing.

1. *Which of these groups of animals change most as they grow?*
   Insects   Birds   Mammals   Fish   Amphibians
2. *What changes do fish, birds, and mammals make as they grow?*

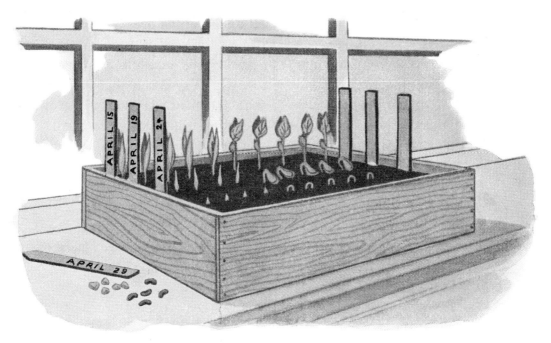

How do plants with seeds begin to grow?

IT IS EASY to watch plants change as they grow if you follow these directions. You will need a box of good soil about four inches deep. Get a handful of bean seeds and a handful of corn seeds. In one end of the box, plant one or two corn seeds. In the other end, plant one or two bean seeds. Then every two or three days for two weeks plant a few more of the two kinds of seeds. Keep the seeds watered and in a sunny place in your schoolroom.

Push little flat sticks part way into the soil beside the seeds. On each stick write the date so that you will know which seeds were planted first. By the time you have planted the last seeds, you will have plants of several different sizes.

Now suppose you try to find out how bean and corn plants grow from the little seeds you planted. If you study the structure of the seeds, you can find out. Soak some seeds in water overnight. Then you can take them apart or cut them open easily, so that you can see the structure of the seeds.

You will learn several things when you take a bean seed apart. You will find that there is an outside coat, like a skin, that easily slips off the wet seed. You will learn that you can split the seed into two parts like the ones in the picture on page 198. When you have done this, study these parts carefully and tell what you see. Use a magnifying glass if you have one.

If you look carefully, you will find something that looks like two little leaves near the end of one half of the bean. There is another part that looks like a tiny stem.

When you look at the corn seed, you will find that it cannot be split in two. So you will have to cut it in two from top to bottom. Down near the pointed end of the corn seed there is a part that looks different from the rest of the seed. You will have to look closely to see it. This part is the beginning of a tiny corn plant. Did you find those parts in the seeds you looked at? Do you see them in the pictures on this page?

The parts you found in the bean seed and in the corn seed are tiny plants

all folded up and ready to grow. The rest of the seed is food for this tiny plant to live on while it is beginning to grow. A seed is really a baby plant with the food that starts it growing and a covering that protects it.

Now you are ready to find out just how the baby plant changes as it begins to grow. Dig up some of the plants from your box of corn and beans. Start with the ones you planted last. Be sure to take plenty of soil with them and wash the soil off after you have dug them up. In this way you will not break the roots of the plants.

Look at your plants carefully and study the pictures on this page. Then make a list of the changes in the plants as they grow taller and taller. Study each plant carefully. See how many changes you can find.

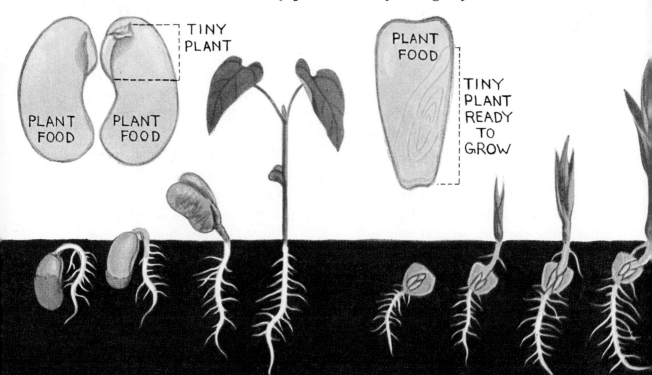

Read the questions on this page. They will help you know what kinds of changes to look for while you are watching your plants grow.

Notice, too, how long it takes a bean or corn seed to grow into a small plant with several leaves. If you plant string-bean seeds in your garden, you can probably pick some beans about seven weeks after you plant them. You can have some radishes three or four weeks after you sow the seeds. Lettuce grows in about six weeks. But if you want to grow some jack-o'-lanterns for Halloween, you will have to sow the seeds about fifteen weeks before you want to pick the pumpkins.

1. *Why did you start growing some bean seeds and some corn seeds on several different days?*
2. *Which part of the plant grows out of the seed first—the root that goes down into the soil or the stem that grows up out of the soil?*
3. *What is happening to the seeds of the plants that have been growing longest? Why?*
4. *What has happened to the covering of the seed?*
5. *What has happened to the food that was inside the seed?*

How do plants grow taller?

ON HIS GRANDFATHER's farm John had often seen a big tree with a rusty old horseshoe nailed to it. When John's father was a boy about ten years old, he nailed that horseshoe to the tree. The tree had grown many feet taller, but the horseshoe was still the same distance from the ground. John could not understand why. He thought that the horseshoe would be moved higher as the tree grew taller.

Do you know why the horseshoe stayed the same distance from the ground? You can use a bean plant from your box of corn and bean plants to help you find out for yourself how trees and other plants grow taller. Choose one of the young growing bean plants and mark the stem between each pair of leaves as shown in the picture. As the bean plant grows taller, mark the stem just below each pair of new leaves.

Does the stem get taller by growing at the bottom or at the top? Do the marks, numbered 1, 2, 3, and 4 in the picture, get farther from the soil? If you do this experiment, you will find that the marks stay in the same place. The stem of the bean plant gets taller by growing at the top.

The horseshoe that John's father nailed to the tree stayed the same distance from the ground even though the tree grew taller. Does this tell you anything about how trees grow tall? Do you think they grow longer all the way along the stem, or *trunk*, or just at the top?

If you look at some twigs and branches in the winter or early spring, you can find out what happens when they grow longer. The picture at the bottom of this page will help you, too. Look at the end of the twig, and you will see the bud. If you open one of these buds, you will find a tiny stem with leaves packed tightly inside. When spring comes, the tiny stem and leaves begin to grow.

When the bud grows, it leaves a ring of rough bark around the twig. If you measure from the bud to the ring below it, you can see how far the twig grew last year. If you measure from this ring to the next ring, you can tell how much the twig grew two years ago. Now you can understand why the horseshoe never got any

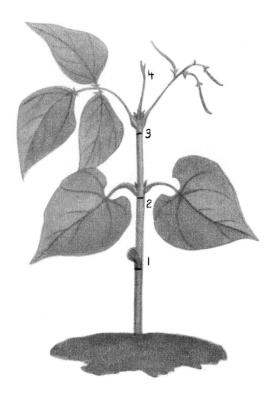

farther from the ground. The trunks of trees and the stems of other plants get taller by growing out from their ends. The branches of trees and other plants get longer by growing out from their ends, too.

---

1. How can you tell how old a twig is?
2. How do plants grow taller? How can you show this?
3. If you hang a swing from the branch of a tree, will the swing get farther from the ground as the tree grows taller? Why?

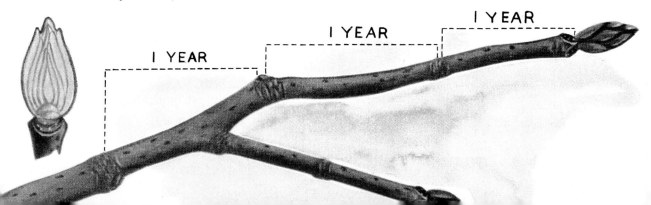

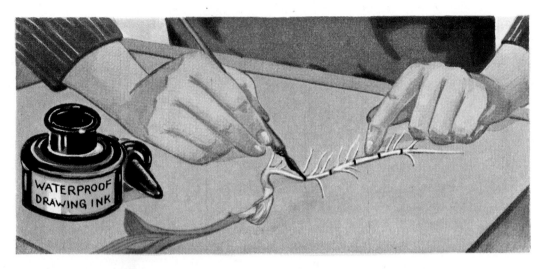

How do the roots of plants grow longer?

NOW YOU CAN use some of your bean or corn plants to help you find out how the roots of plants grow. Take two or three of your biggest plants and pull them up carefully so that you will not break the roots. Wash the roots clean. Get a kind of ink that cannot be washed off by water and make marks on the roots. Begin very near the tip. Put a ruler alongside each root and make the marks the same distance apart all the way up to the top of the root. Now put the plants into a box of moist sawdust. It will be easy to pull the plants out of the sawdust to study them again. Be sure to keep the sawdust moist.

Some boys and girls in a science class tried this experiment once. Of course, they wondered what was going to happen to the marks. But they had to wait more than a week for the plants to grow. At last, the day came to pull them up and look at them. At first, no one saw anything interesting. The marks were all there. Then Charley noticed something.

"This root has grown way out beyond the bottom mark," he said.

By this time Peggy had noticed something else. "The two marks nearest the end of the root are farther apart," she said. "But the other marks are almost exactly the same distance apart as when we made them."

The picture on the next page shows what the boys and girls saw. What does it show about how roots grow? The class decided that roots get longer by growing at the end. The last mark they had put on each root had been almost at the tip. Now the

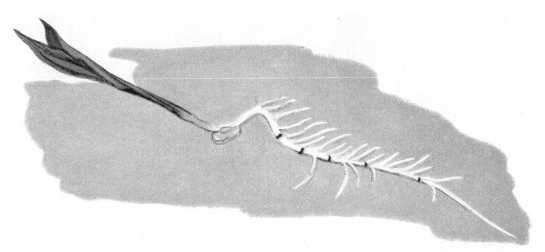

mark was much farther back from the tip. The root had grown an inch longer at its end. Between the two lowest marks it was a little longer than it had been. But the other marks on the root were almost the same distance apart as when they were made.

Roots can grow like this until they are very long. Sometimes the roots of a tree grow to be more than 50 feet long. Some of the roots of a tree in your yard may be growing under your neighbor's lawn.

Roots have branches, too. The branches also get longer by growing out at their tips. When you pull up a large plant, you see that it has many, many roots. They branch and grow out in all directions from the plant. If you could take all the roots of one full-grown wheat plant and put them together in a string, you might have a string that is several hundred feet long.

A sugar beet may send roots down five or six feet into the soil. One scientist measured all the roots of an oak tree. The tree had 450 feet of roots. You probably never thought that such a big part of a plant may be under the soil.

Did you ever try to pull up different kinds of weeds? It is easy to pull up some kinds and hard to pull up others. If the ground is dry, it is almost impossible to pull up a dandelion or a burdock. But plantain and chickweed pull up easily. If you can do so, dig up four or five kinds of weeds and study the roots.

If you dig up a dandelion, you find that it has one big main root that goes straight down. So does a burdock. But goldenrod and daisy plants have a bunch of slender roots that grow out sideways. Tree roots grow in the same two ways. Some trees, such as the white oak, have a big

When the soil is cut away, you can see how long the roots of the trees are.

main root. It goes straight down. Of course, it has roots that grow out sideways, too. Other trees do not have a main root that grows straight down. All their roots grow out sideways.

It is a great help to plants to have roots that can grow far down and out in all directions. These roots help plants get the water and materials for making food. Later in your science work, you will learn how roots take in water and materials for making food from the soil. You will also learn how plants make food from these materials.

How do the stems of plants get thicker?

OF COURSE, you know that the stems and even the roots of plants get thicker as well as longer. But you may be surprised to learn how they get thicker. Can you find a piece of tree trunk that has been sawed across? Perhaps you have a woodpile at home where you can find a piece like this. Get a piece that has not been split.

Two of the boys in the science class said that they could find some pieces to bring to school. The next day the boys and girls looked at the structure of the inside of the branches and the trunk of a small tree. The picture on this page shows what the inside of a tree trunk looks like. Do you see the rings of light-colored and dark-colored wood? The rings show you how the tree grows thicker. It grows thicker by adding layers of wood around the outside just underneath the bark. Each ring is made of two layers of wood. Branches of plants grow thicker in this way, too.

The layer of wood that grows in the spring looks light-colored. The layer that grows in the summer looks dark. In this way a light layer and a dark

These huge trees in California are hundreds of years old.

layer are added to the tree trunk every year.

What can the layers tell you about a tree? Do you see that they can tell you how old it is? Every year one ring of new wood is added. Each ring has a dark layer and a light layer. The class counted the dark layers in one piece of tree trunk that the boys had brought. The tree was twenty-eight years old. Another tree was twenty years old. Count the dark layers in the picture on page 205. How old was the tree?

Perhaps you are wondering how many years trees keep on making rings like this. Some trees grow more slowly and live much longer than others. They can keep on making rings for hundreds of years. But as they grow older, they make new wood more slowly. So the rings are thinner.

Do you live in the western part of our country? Or have you taken a trip to see the big trees in California? Perhaps you have driven through a tunnel that was cut right through one of these big trees.

It takes a long time for a tree to grow big. But it can be cut down in just a few minutes. Think about that if you see someone chopping down a fine large tree. Probably that tree has been living longer than you have. If it is allowed to go on grow-ing, it will give shade on the hot days. It will make homes for birds. Its roots will help keep the soil from being blown and washed away. It will help make our country a more beautiful place to live in.

Some parts of the world have been almost ruined because all the trees were cut down. Then there were no tree roots to keep the soil from being blown or washed away. When all the good soil was gone, the people could not grow crops for themselves or their animals. Soon very few people could live there. We must be very careful that this does not happen in our country. You can see why we must save, or *conserve*, our trees and use them wisely.

Many plants do not grow in the way that trees grow. They do not get thicker by adding layers of wood around the trunk and branches. Corn is a plant like this. The boys and girls in one science class decided to see what the inside of a cornstalk looks like. They cut a cornstalk into pieces crosswise. Soon Mary said, "I can't find any rings inside like the ones we saw in the tree."

Mary was right. There are no rings in the cornstalk, as you can see from

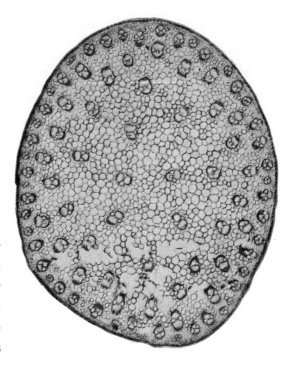

This is how the inside of a cornstalk looks when you see it through a microscope.

the picture on this page. The corn plant gets thicker by growing all through the inside. This shows us another way in which plants grow thicker. Not all kinds of plants add new layers around the stem and branches. Look again at the picture on page 205 and compare it with the picture on this page. Do you see how differently the stems of the two plants grow thicker?

---

1. *What are the two different ways in which plants grow thicker?*
2. *How can you tell how old a tree was when it was cut down?*
3. *Why must we conserve our trees?*

In what directions do the parts of plants grow?

WHEN YOU PLANTED your corn and bean seeds, did you look to see which was the bottom and which was the top of the seed? No, you probably just put the seeds into the soil without thinking about that at all. When the seeds started to grow, the roots of all the plants grew downward into the soil. And the stems grew up and soon were above the soil. Do roots always grow down? Do stems always grow up?

Here is an experiment that will show you something about how roots grow. Line a glass with moist blotting paper as shown in the picture on this page. Then fill the glass with moist sawdust or sand. Soak a dozen corn seeds overnight. Then put them between the sides of the glass and the blotting paper. Plant the seeds about an inch apart. Put the glass in a warm place and keep the sawdust or sand moist but not too wet.

After a few days look at the seeds. Which way do the roots of the little plants grow? After the roots have grown about an inch long, take half of the plants out of the glass and put them back so that the roots point upward. Watch the roots for two or three days. What do they do?

The roots of the plants that were left in the glass kept growing downward.

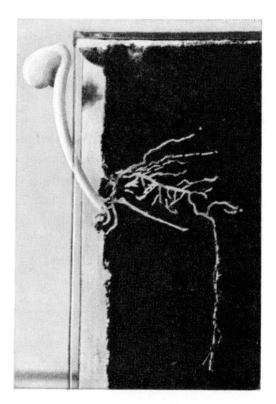

When the roots of the other plants were turned so that they pointed up, they turned around and began to grow downward again. No matter in what direction a root may point when it starts growing, it will always turn and grow downward.

Now look again at the plants in the glass. What has happened to their stems? The stems of the plants that had been left in the glass kept on growing upward. But the stems of the plants that were turned down have turned around and are now growing upward again.

In the picture on the right on page 208 is a young bean plant. After it had grown awhile, it was turned on its side. What happened to the roots and the stem of the bean plant?

Here is another experiment that will show you how stems grow. Get three small geranium plants. Choose plants that are growing well in small flowerpots. Cut two pieces of wire screen to fit around the stems of two of the plants and over the tops of the flowerpots. Fasten the screen on with wire. This will keep the soil from falling out during the experiment.

Water the plants. Now take one of the plants with the screen over it and lay it on its side. Hang the other one up so that its stem is pointing downward, as the picture on this page shows. Keep the third plant with its stem pointing up.

Water all three plants whenever they need it and watch them for several weeks. In what direction does the stem of the plant that was pointing up grow? What has happened to the stems of the other two plants? They have turned and are now growing upward.

If you did the experiment with the corn seeds, you found out that roots always grow downward. This helps them get water and other materials from the soil. Roots do another interesting thing that helps them get water. If another part of the soil has more water than the part where the plant is growing, the roots will grow toward the part where there is more water.

Sometimes water is deep down in the soil. Then the roots keep on growing down until they reach the water. Sometimes there is water just on one side of the roots. Then the roots will grow toward the side where this water is. You can see that roots do this if you try this experiment. First, find a small unpainted flowerpot. Plug the drain hole with a rubber stopper and sealing wax. Set this empty flowerpot in the middle of a box about two feet square. Fill the box around the flowerpot with rich soil.

Soak some bean seeds overnight. Plant several bean seeds near the pot and several seeds farther away from it. The soil should be moist when the seeds are planted. Now pour water into the flowerpot. It will slowly pass through the sides of the pot into the soil that is near it. Do not water the soil in any other way.

Your box of soil with the flowerpot to hold the water should look like this. The beans will probably look like these plants when they are several inches high.

Now find another box of the same size. Put the same kind of rich soil in it but do not set a flowerpot in the box. Plant the same kind of seeds in this box and plant them in the same way. Water the plants by sprinkling water on top of the soil. The only difference between the two boxes is in the way the roots get water. If there is any difference in the way the roots grow, the reason for the difference will be the way the plants get water.

After the plants are several inches high, dig up some of them that are growing near the flowerpot. Be sure to notice in which direction the roots are growing. Now dig up some of the plants farther from the flowerpot. In which direction do their roots grow? Last of all, look at the roots of the plants in the box without the flowerpot. How are they different from the other roots?

You can use what you have learned to explain what happened in this story. Some people built a house in a grove of poplar trees. They put tile pipe in the ground to carry waste water from their house to the sewer under the street. After a few years they began to have trouble. The waste water would no longer flow in the pipe from the house. It even backed up and flowed out on the basement floor.

When they dug down to the tile pipe, they found that the roots of the trees had grown through the joints. The roots had grown so big that they had filled the pipe and broken some of it. Why did the roots grow into the tile pipe?

Here is another experiment. It will show you another interesting thing about the way plants grow. Find a small cardboard box just large enough to hold a shallow dish. The box should be about three inches deep. Cut a hole in one side of the box so that light can get in. Now put several pieces of moist blotting paper in the bottom of the dish. Lay a dozen or more bean, radish, or grass seeds on the moist paper. Cover the box. Be sure to use good seeds and keep them moist. In what direction do the stems grow?

If you did the experiment carefully, you found that the stems grow toward the light that came through the hole in the side of the box. If the distance is not too great, the stems may even grow out through the hole.

You can try another experiment if you have some plants. Use a small geranium or any kind of house plant. Put it in a window for a few days. Notice how the leaves turn. After most of the large leaves have turned toward the light, turn the plant around so that the leaves face the

room. Now watch the plant again. How long does it take for the leaves to turn toward the light? Try putting a whole plant in a box that has a hole in it. What happens to the leaves?

You know that plant roots will grow toward water. Now you see that plant stems and leaves will grow toward light. If a plant is shaded on one side and has the sunlight on the other side, it will grow more on the sunny side. Plants even grow with their leaves arranged to catch the most sunlight. Study the pictures on this page to see how the leaves are growing to catch the light. Then look at a vine to see how its leaves are turned to catch the light.

---

1. *How can you show that the root of a plant always grows down and the stem always grows up?*
2. *How do the directions in which the roots and stems grow help plants stay alive?*
3. *Do stems of plants grow toward or away from the light?*
4. *Do roots grow toward water in soil or away from water?*

1. The picture on this page shows how a mosquito changes as it grows. Find the four stages of its life.

2. Make a list of animals that change as they grow. Let each boy and girl choose one animal. Then have each one answer these questions about the animal. How does it change as it grows? What helps it grow? What food does it use?

3. Try to tell the story shown in the picture on these pages: 186-187 (Monarch butterfly), pages 188-189 (Cecropia moth), page 190 (grasshopper and cricket), pages 192-193 (frog).

4. In Unit One you learned different ways to make discoveries. Which of these ways have you used in this unit?

5. Where would you look to find these things—toads' eggs, Monarch butterfly eggs, grasshopper eggs, mosquito eggs, tadpoles?

6. How is the way plants grow like the way animals grow? How is it different?

7. Make a list of things that happen as a seed grows into a plant.

8. How does knowing about the structure of a seed help you understand how it grows into a plant?

9. Make a list of all of the animals and all of the plants mentioned in this unit. Then put them into the groups you learned in Unit One.

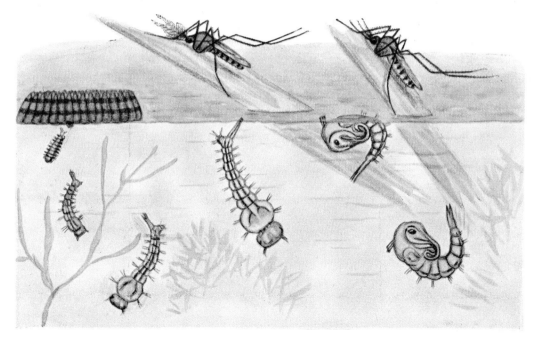

1. Look for cocoons on trees and bushes. Keep them to find out what comes from them.

2. Bring some caterpillars to school and watch to see if they spin a cocoon or make a chrysalis. Keep the cocoon or chrysalis and find out what happens to it.

3. Examine an ant's nest. See if you can find the four stages of an ant's life.

4. Find pictures in books and magazines that show how animals change as they grow.

5. Have an exhibit of baby pets.

6. Find some young grasshoppers. Put them in a cage and feed them grass. Watch what happens when they grow.

7. Make some cuttings of house plants. Plant them in moist sand. Keep a record of how they change as they grow.

8. To see how leaves grow, draw a mark across a narcissus leaf. Measure from the bottom of the leaf up to the mark. Then measure it again in a week. What does this show you about how narcissus leaves grow?

9. Get a geranium plant. Hold a piece of paper against a new leaf and draw the outline of the leaf. Keep the drawing. In a week or so draw the outline of the leaf again. Use the same piece of paper. What does this show you about how geranium leaves grow?

10. Visit a garden or greenhouse and try to see some of the things you have learned about in this unit.

11. Try to find pictures of big trees in different parts of our country.

12. Keep a record of the way an ivy plant grows. With a yardstick measure the length of a branch. Make a drawing of it beside the yardstick. Write the date on your drawing. Three or four weeks later measure the ivy branch again. Add to your first drawing any new parts that have grown. Then write a story of how the ivy plant grew. Tell where the stem grew longer and where new leaves were added.

SCIENCE WORDS

Can you say the word *chrysalis*? Do you know what it means? You can easily find out. Look in the list of science words that begins on this page. The word *chrysalis* is on the next page.

Notice that each word in the list is printed two times. The second time shows you how to say the word. Some of the letters have marks over them. The mark tells how the letter sounds. Look in the list below to see how each letter sounds.

Now look at the word *backbone* on this page. The slanting mark ′ after *bak* is bigger than the slanting mark ′ after *bōn*. So you say *bak* with more force than *bōn*.

a	hat, cap	èr	term, learn
ā	age, face	i	it, pin
ã	care, air	ī	ice, five
ä	father, far	o	hot, rock
e	let, best	ō	open, go
ē	equal, see		

ô	order, all	ə represents:	
u	cup, butter	a	in about
ù	full, put	e	in taken
ü	rule, move	i	in pencil
ū	use, music	o	in lemon
		u	in circus

al ni co mag net (al′ni kō mag′nit), a magnet made of aluminum, nickel, cobalt, and iron. It will pick up things that are heavier than it is.

am phib i an (am fib′i ən), a cold-blooded animal that lives in water and breathes with gills when young but that has lungs and can live on land when grown up.

an ten na (an ten′ə), a feeler on the head of an insect and some other animals.

an ten nae (an ten′ē), more than one antenna.

a quar i um (ə kwãr′i əm), a tank or glass bowl where fish, other water animals, and water plants are kept.

ar ma dil lo (är′mə dil′ō), a small mammal with a hard, bony shell. It has only a little hair.

at tract (ə trakt′), pull toward itself. A magnet attracts iron and steel.

ax is (ak′sis), a real or imaginary line around which something turns. The earth turns around an axis.

back bone (bak′bōn′), the long row of bones along the back of the body.

Be tel geuse (bē′təl jüz), a large reddish star in the constellation Orion.

Big Dip per (big dip′ər), a group of stars in the constellation Ursa Major.

blood ves sel (blud ves′əl), a tube in the body through which blood flows.

brain (brān), the part of the body inside the skull. It is used for thinking and for directing the other parts of the body. Nerves run to and from the brain.

car bon di ox ide (kär′bən dī ok′sīd), a gas that is made of carbon and oxygen. It cannot be seen or smelled.

car ti lage (kär′ti lij), firm, tough material that forms parts of the skeleton.

Cas si o pe ia (kas′i ō pē′ə), a constellation in the northern sky.

cen ti pede (sen′ti pēd), a small worm-like animal with many pairs of legs.

chrys a lis (kris′ə lis), a hard case made by a caterpillar to live in while it is becoming a butterfly.

co coon (kə kün′), a silky case made by a caterpillar to live in while it is becoming a moth.

cold-blood ed (kōld′ blud′ id), having blood whose temperature changes with the temperature of the surroundings.

com pass (kum′pəs), an instrument to tell direction.

con dense (kən dens′), change from a gas to a liquid.

con stel la tion (kon′stə lā′shən), a group of stars.

de cay (di kā′), rot or spoil.

des ert (dez′ərt), a dry region with few kinds of plants and animals.

di gest (di jest′ or dī jest′), change food in the stomach and intestines so that the body can use it.

dis solve (di zolv′), change into a liquid by mixing with a liquid. Sugar and salt dissolve in water.

ear drum (ēr′drum′), a thin part inside the ear that makes hearing possible.

e vap o rate (i vap′ə rāt), change from a liquid into a gas.

ex per i ment (eks per′i ment), test to try to find out something.

fawn (fôn), a deer less than a year old.

fer ti liz er (fèr′ti līz′ər), a material that is mixed with soil to help plants grow.

flow er (flou′ər), the part of a plant that makes the seeds.

force (fōrs), a pull or push.

gas (gas), a material like air; neither a solid nor a liquid.

ge o graph ic poles (jē′ə graf′ik pōlz), the poles at the ends of the earth's axis.

germ (jèrm), a very tiny plant or animal that can cause a disease.

gills (gilz), the parts of a fish and some other animals that are used for getting air from water.

gris tle (gris′əl), cartilage.

heart (härt), a large, hollow muscle that pumps the blood through the body.

in sect (in′sekt), a small, cold-blooded animal with six legs whose body is divided into three parts.

in tes tine (in tes′tin), a long tube into which food goes from the stomach.

jel ly fish (jel′i fish′), a water animal whose soft body is made of a clear, jelly-like material.

joint (joint), the place where two bones are joined together so that they can move.

Ju pi ter (jü′pi tər), 1. the largest planet. 2. the king of the gods in old stories.

large in tes tine (lärj in tes′tin), a tube connected with the small intestine. Food that has not been digested passes out of the body from the large intestine.

lig a ment (lig′ə mənt), a strong band that connects bones or holds parts of the body in place.

liq uid (lik′wid), a material like water; neither a solid nor a gas.

Lit tle Dip per (lit′əl dip′ər), a group of stars in the constellation Ursa Minor.

liv ing (liv′ing), alive now or alive at one time.

lode stone (lōd′stōn′), a kind of rock that attracts iron and steel just as a magnet does.

lungs (lungz), the parts through which air gets into the bodies of many animals.

mag net (mag′nit), a piece of iron, steel, or other material that attracts other pieces of iron or steel.

mag net ic (mag net′ik), attracted by a magnet.

mag net ize (mag′ni tīz), make into a magnet.

mag no li a (mag nō′li ə), a tree with large white, pink, or purplish flowers.

mam mal (mam′əl), a warm-blooded animal that has fur or hair. The mother feeds its young with milk from its own body.

Mars (märz), the planet between the earth and Jupiter.

Mer cu ry (mėr′kū ri), the planet nearest to the sun.

me te or (mē′ti ər), mass of rock or metal that falls through the sky toward the earth. It is often called a shooting star.

me te or ite (mē′ti ər īt), a piece of a meteor that has fallen to the earth.

mi cro scope (mī′krə skōp), an instrument that makes very small things look larger.

molt (mōlt), shed skin or feathers.

moth (môth), an insect that looks much like a butterfly but has a heavier body and feathery feelers.

mus cles (mus′əlz), the parts of the body that are fastened to the bones and make them move.

Nep tune (nep′tūn), the large planet that is next to the farthest from the sun.

nerves (nėrvz), the white threadlike parts of the body that carry messages to and from the brain in all parts of the body.

non-liv ing (non liv′ing), not alive now and never alive.

non-mag net ic (non′mag net′ik), not attracted by a magnet.

O ri on (ō rī′ən), a constellation in the southern sky.

ox y gen (ok′si jən), a gas that makes up part of the air. It cannot be seen or smelled.

pas teur ize (pas′tər īz), heat hot enough and long enough to kill germs.

per spi ra tion (pėr′spi rā′shən), sweat.

plan et (plan′it), one of the big balls that move around the sun. The earth is a planet.

Plu to (plü′tō), the planet farthest from the sun.

Po lar is (pō lär′is), a name for the North Star, or the Pole Star.

pole (pōl), 1. either end of the earth's axis. 2. one of the two places on a magnet where its force is strongest.

por cu pine (pôr′kū pīn), a mammal whose body is covered with spines or quills.

pore (pōr), a very small opening in the skin through which sweat comes out of the body.

pos ture (pos′chər), a way of holding the body.

pu pil (pū′pəl), the black spot in the center of the eye through which light gets into the eye.

re flect (ri flekt′), throw back.

re pel (ri pel′), push away from itself.

rep tile (rep′til or rep′tĭl), a cold-blooded animal whose body is covered with scales. It has lungs for breathing.

re volve (ri volv′), move in a circle.

Ri gel (rī′jəl), a large, bright star in the constellation Orion.

ro tate (rō′tāt), turn around an axis.

sal a man der (sal′ə man′dər),   an amphibian that is shaped like a lizard.

sa li va (sə lĭ′və),   the liquid in the mouth that helps dissolve food.

sap (sap),   the liquid that travels through a plant and carries dissolved minerals and food.

Sat urn (sat′ərn),   the large planet that has rings around it.

scales (skālz),   the thin, flat pieces of hard material that fit over one another to make the skin of reptiles and most fishes.

sci en tist (sĭ′ən tist),   a person who spends his life studying science.

sea son (sē′zən),   spring, summer, autumn, or winter.

sea ur chin (sē ėr′chin),   a small, round sea animal with a spiny shell.

sen ses (sen′siz),   seeing, hearing, smelling, touching, and tasting.   Your eyes, ears, nose, etc., give your body the sense of sight, the sense of sound, the sense of smell, etc.

skel e ton (skel′i tən),   1. the framework of bones in the body.   2. the hard outside covering of an insect's body.

skull (skul),   the rounded covering of bones in the head.   It protects the brain.

small in tes tine (smôl in tes′tin),   the part of the intestine connected with the stomach.   Most of the food digests there.

sol id (sol′id),   a material that keeps its shape; neither a liquid nor a gas.

spi nal cord (spĭ′nəl kôrd),   a long white cord that runs through the center of the backbone.

spine (spīn),   the backbone.

spore (spōr),   a tiny part of a plant that grows into a new plant.   Some plants have spores instead of seeds.

stage (stāj),   one step in the growth of something.

star (stär),   a big ball of glowing gases that looks like a bright point in the sky at night.

star fish (stär′fish′),   a sea animal with five arms.

stom ach (stum′ək),   the part of the body where food goes to be mixed and changed so that the body can use it.

struc ture (struk′chər),   the parts of anything and the way they are put together.

symp tom (simp′təm),   a sign that something is wrong with a person's body and that he is sick.

tel e scope (tel′i skōp),   an instrument that makes things far away look nearer.

ther mom e ter (thər mom′i tər),   an instrument that measures how hot something is.

trunk (trungk),   the main stem of a tree.

U ra nus (ūr′ə nəs),   the planet between Saturn and Neptune.

Ur sa Ma jor (ėr′sə mā′jər),   the Big Bear, a constellation in the northern sky. The Big Dipper is in Ursa Major.

Ur sa Mi nor (ėr′sə mĭ′nər),   the Little Bear, a constellation in the northern sky. The Little Dipper is in Ursa Minor.

va por (vā′pər),   a gas, such as water vapor, made from a liquid or a solid.

Ve nus (vē′nəs),   the brightest planet.

vi ta min (vĭ′tə min),   one of the materials in food that the body needs to grow properly and to protect it from certain diseases.

warm-blood ed (wôrm′blud′id),   having blood whose temperature stays about the same all the time.

wind pipe (wind′pīp′),   the tube that carries air to and from the lungs.

INDEX

IN THE NEXT FEW PAGES is a list of things that your book tells about. This list is called an *index*. You can use the index to help you find things in your book.

Notice that all the words beginning with *A* come first. All words that begin with *B* come next. Find the words that begin with *S*.

Suppose that you want to find out what kind of animal a cat is. First, look for *cat* in the index. What pages in your book tell about cats? Look at page 12 and find out what it tells you about cats. What does page 20 tell you? Does page 21 tell you what kind of animal a cat is?

Does glass belong to the group of living things or to the group of non-living things? Find the pages in your book that tell you.

A star after a number (like 29*) means that there is a picture on that page. What page has a picture of a cat? What pages have pictures of frogs?

678910111213141516171819202122232425 605958575655